Common Core State Standards

3rd Grade Lesson Plans

Language Arts & Math

Teacher's Life

www.myteacherslife.com

Follow us on Twitter, Facebook and Pinterest – Teachers Life, LLC

Table of Contents

Recommended Reading

Fiction

*2030: A Day in the Life
of Tomorrow's Kids* by Amy Zuckerman and Jim Daly, illustrated by John Manders
Best Friends for Frances by Russell Hoban, illustrated by Lillian Hoban
The Facts and Fictions of Minna Pratt by Patricia MacLachlan
George and Martha by James Marshall
Hedgie's Surprise by Jan Brett
Shipwrecked! The True Adventures of a Japanese Boy by Rhoda Blumberg
The Tale of Despereaux by Kate DiCamillo
Grk and the Pelotti Gang by Joshua Doder
The Whipping Boy by Sid Fleischman
Where the Mountain Meets the Moon by Grace Lin
I Was a Third Grade Spy by Mary Jane Auch
Soupy Saturdays with the Pain and the Great One by Judy Blume
Dexter the Tough by Margaret Peterson Haddix
Remembering Mrs. Rossi by Amy Hest
Alvin Ho: Allergic to Girls, and other Scary Things by Lenore Look
Adventures of Ali Baba Bernstein – Hurwitz, Johanna
The Disappearing Cookies and Other Cases – Simon, Seymour
Third Grade Stars – Ransom, Candice
The Kings Equal – Paterson, Katherine
Foolish Gretel – Armstrong, Jennifer

Series

Snarf Attack, Underfoodle, and the Secret of Life (Riot Brothers series) by Mary Amato
Ruby and the Booker Boys (series) by Derrick Barnes
Spiderwick Chronicles (series) by Holly Black and Tony DiTerlizzi
Allie Finkle's Rules for Girls (series) by Meg Cabot
Ramona the Pest (series) by Beverly Cleary
Phineas L. MacGuire (series) by Frances O'Roark Dowell
My Weird School (series) by Dan Gutman
Just Grace (series) by Charise Harper
Piper Reed (series) by Kimberly Willis Holt
Gooney Bird Greene (series) by Lois Lowry

Non-Fiction

Amelia to Zora: Twenty-six Women Who Changed the World by Cynthia Chin-Lee, illustrated by Megan Halsey and Sean Addy
Author: A True Story by Helen Lester
Bill Peet: An Autobiography written and illustrated by Bill Peet

Clean Sea: Story of Rachel Carson by Carol Hilgartner Schlank, Barbara Metzger, illustrated by David Katz

Houdini: World's Greatest Mystery Man and Escape King by Kathleen Krull, illustrated by Eric Velasquez

The American Story: 100 True Tales from American History by Jennifer Armstrong, illustrated by Roger Roth

Animals in the House: A History of Pets and People by Sheila Keenan

So You Want to Be President? by Judith St. George, illustrated by David Small

What if You Met a Pirate? By Jan Adkins

Easy to Be Green: Simple Activities You Can Do to Save the Earth by Ellie O'Ryan, illustrated by Ivanke & Lola

Great White Sharks by Sandra Markle, illustrated with photographs

Polar Bears and the Arctic (Magic Tree House Research Guides) by Mary Pope Osborne

365 Ways to Live Green for Kids: Saving the Environment at Home, School, or at Play — Every Day! by Sheri Amsel

Hey Batta Batta Swing! The Wild Old Days of Baseball by Sally Cook and James Charlton, illustrated by Ross MacDonald

Ultimate Chess by Jon Tremaine

The Story of Kwanzaa by Donna L. Washington, illustrated by Stephen Taylor

Ballet for Martha by Jan Greenberg, Sandra Jordan

It's a Dog's Life: How Man's Best Friend Sees, Hears, and Smells the World by Susan E. Goodman

Minette's Feast: The Delicious Story of Julia Child and Her Cat by Susanna Reich

The Notorious Benedict by Arnold Steve Sheinkin

Rah, rah, radishes! : a vegetable chant by April Pulley Sayre

Poetry

Dont Read This Book Whatever You Do: More Poems About School by Kalli Dakos

If Kids Ruled the School by Bruce Lansky

Sad Underwear and Other Complications: More Poems fo Children and Their Parents by Judith Viorst

Waiting to See the Principal and Other Poems by Joe Sottile

Rainy Day Poems by James McDonald

Where the Sidewalk Ends by Shel Silverstein

When We Were Very Young by A.A. Milne

A Light in the Attic by Shel Silverstein

The New Kid on the Block by Jack Prelutsky

Love That Dog by Sharon Creech

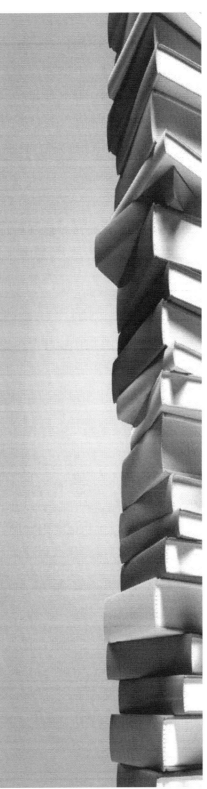

Language Arts

Lesson One

Title: Colorful Questioning

Topic: Answering questions from a provided reading or text.

Objective of lesson: Students will correctly answer questions based on a text.

Common Core State Standard used: RL 3.1 Ask and answer questions to demonstrate understanding of a text, referring explicitly to the text as the basis for the answers.

Materials needed: Colored popsicle sticks or a color wheel with spinner

Text

Colored paper/Drawing paper

List of appropriate questions for the text

Time for lesson: 30 -45 minutes - depending on text

Lesson:

- Allow students to group themselves into small groups of three or four.
- Choose a color to represent each group and have them write out a card or provide a slip of paper in the appropriate color.
- After reading a text of any type spin the dial or draw a stick and ask that color group to answer the question.
- To alter the setup the teams can keep scores and earn extra points based on score or students can choose which type of question the group wants (who, what, when, where, why, how).

Assessment: Depending on whether score is kept or not, students can be assessed on participation, correct answers, and team work.

Lesson Two

Title: Question Your Partner

Topic: Answering and creating questions from a provided reading or text

Objective of lesson: Students will correctly answer and create questions based on a text.

Common Core State Standard used: RL 3.1 Ask and answer questions to demonstrate understanding of a text, referring explicitly to the text as the basis for the answers.

Materials needed: Paper

Pencil

Highlighter (per pair)

Text

Time for lesson: 30 – 45 minutes – depending on text

Lesson:

- After reading or allowing students to read a text, explain that they are going to create their own quiz.
- Have students write 3-5 questions each based on the text. (prompt students to create who, what, when, where, why, and how questions)
- Explain that the questions need to have clear answers, but be challenging. Provide an example if necessary.
- Allow students time to write the questions, than find a partner. The partners will ask each other the questions to make sure they are appropriate.
- Next have the partners choose three of their best questions combined and highlight.
- Share and review the questions with the class.
- Collect the highlighted questions and turn them into a quiz on the story. Use only questions written by the students.

- Give the quiz the following day or during the same week.

Assessment: Score quizzes as a normal test would be graded as an assessment.

Lesson One

Title: Paint Me a Story

Topic: Recounting stories

Objective of lesson: Students will recount a story as art in a small group.

Common Core State Standard used: RL 3.2 Recount stories, including fables, folktales, and myths from diverse cultures; determine the central message, lesson, or moral and explain how it is conveyed through key details in the text.

Materials needed: Butcher paper

Pencils

Art supplies (markers, paint, crayons) and: Henny Penny by Paul Galdone

Time for lesson: 30-45 minutes

Lesson:

- Read the text or have students read the text Henny Penny as a group.

- Allow students to view the pictures and discuss each scene as it occurs (The acorn falling, telling each animal, the walking as a group)

- Explain to students that they are going to recreate the book in art, no words allowed.

- Allow students to work in groups to create a large storyboard/comic strip of the book Henny Penny on butcher paper. Remind students that neatness counts and each important scene should be illustrated in order. (Alternate choice: Write scenes on slips of paper, have students draw a scene and then illustrate it, have students work together to put the 'storyboard' up on a wall in logical order.)

- Display the story boards.

Assessment: Creation of distinct scenes as a group (or individuals), in logical order should be graded. See rubric.

Lesson Two

Title: ReenACTments

Topic: Recounting stories

Objective of lesson: Students will recount the moral or lesson in a story through imagination and acting out of scenes

Common Core State Standard used: RL 3.2 Recount stories, including fables, folktales, and myths from diverse cultures; determine the central message, lesson, or moral and explain how it is conveyed through key details in the text.

Materials needed: Writing paper

Pencils

Art supplies (markers, paint, crayons)

Text: Story with a strong lesson or moral

Time for lesson: 60-120 minutes

Lesson:

- After reading or listening to a story, discuss what can be learned from the story.

- Explain to students that using the same lesson, they will work in small groups to create a scene, with dialogue, to teach the same lesson.

- Allow students to group themselves in groups of 3-5. Explain that all people must participate and basic props can be used or made. Each skit should last about 5-10 minutes.

- Allow each group to perform the skit.

Assessment: See rubric.

Lesson One

Title: Sam Stories

Topic: Character traits

Objective of lesson: Students will create a depiction of a character based on gender neutral traits.

Common Core State Standard used: RL 3.3 Describe characters in a story (e.g., their traits, motivations, or feelings) and explain how their actions contribute to the sequence of events

Materials needed: Sample 'Sam' story

Pencil

Art supplies (paper, crayons, markers, paint)

Time for lesson: 20-30 minutes

Lesson:

- Have students discuss how we know a boy from a girl (generically speaking) in a story. What if we only have a name? How would we know the difference? Sometimes we must base our opinions on what we know and they may differ from person to person.

- Read students the Sam text (included).

- Have students draw a picture of what they believe Sam looks like. Remind student that Sam can be short for Sammy or Samantha or Samuel.

- Have students write one or two sentences on the back as to why they think Sam looks a certain way.

- Display 'Sam's' pictures if possible.

Assessment: A neat depiction of Sam and logical reasoning behind the choices. *The goal is to help students realize people have different perceptions and each can be correct if the character is not clearly defined.

"Sam"

Sam is an excellent student. Sam loves going to class, but the favorite part of Sam's day is recess. Sam loves to run and play kickball, but when the weather is bad, Sam likes to play dress-up in the classroom. After school Sam attends dance classes two days a week and soccer practice two other days. On the weekends, Sam loves to have friends over to play basketball or play video games. Sam is an active child.

Lesson Two

Title: Emotional Squares

Topic: Character emotion recognition

Objective of lesson: Students will recognize basic emotions of a given character.

Common Core State Standard used: RL 3.3 Describe characters in a story (e.g., their traits, motivations, or feelings) and explain how their actions contribute to the sequence of events

Materials needed: Text: Goosebumps series: I Live in Your Basement by R.L. Stine

Five square strip (included)

Crayons

Time for lesson: 15-30 minutes (per session)

Lesson:

- Lesson can be taught in sections or as a lengthy story time. Have students listen to a chapter or the full book as a read aloud.

- As the book is read, at random times, ask students how a specific character may be feeling (happy, sad, scared, tired, angry).

- Have students display the emotion they feel the character is feeling. Discuss any differences that occur.

Assessment: Monitor students to see if correct emotions and/or reactions are identified as evidenced by the correct face showing on the square strip.

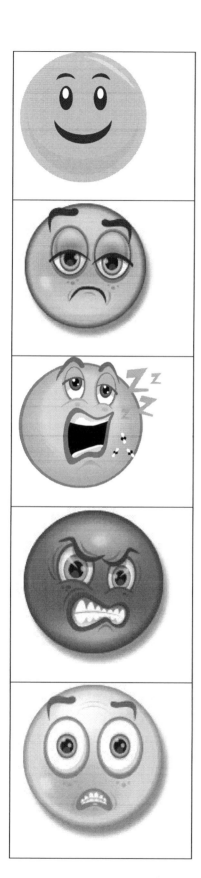

Lesson One

Title: The Literal Meaning

Topic: Literal versus non-literal meanings

Objective of lesson: Students will demonstrate the differences between literal and non-literal meanings.

Common Core State Standard used: RL 3.4 Determine the meaning of words and phrases as they are used in a text, distinguishing literal from non-literal language.

Materials needed: List of figurative statements

Large paper

Crayons/markers/pencils

Time for lesson: 20 - 30 minutes

Lesson:

- Have students fold a sheet of paper into eight equal sections.

- Provide a written list (on the board) of several figurative statements. Explain to students that often sayings have different meanings than what the individual words actually say. This is figurative language or a non-literal meaning. Use the familiar example of a strong rain and people saying 'it is raining cats and dogs'. It is not literally raining cats and dogs.

- Have students choose four figurative statements. For each statement have the student write the statement and label a block as literal or non-literal.

- Next have students illustrate each phrase as figurative or literal. (Draw it actually raining cats and dogs vs. a harsh rain storm)

Assessment: See rubric for artwork also add points for appropriate illustration of literal vs. figurative.

Lesson Two

Title: That Makes Nonsense

Topic: Understanding unfamiliar words in text

Objective of lesson: Students will demonstrate ability to identify unknown nonsense words by meaning through the use of replacement words.

Common Core State Standard used: RL 3.4 Determine the meaning of words and phrases as they are used in a text, distinguishing literal from non-literal language.

Materials needed: Sample paragraphs with nonsense words

Writing paper

Pencils

Time for lesson: 15-25 minutes

Lesson:

- Offer students a copy of the included paragraphs or project a single copy for all students.

- Explain to students that there are nonsense words sprinkled in the paragraph that need to be replaced by real words.

- As students read, have them to replace the nonsense words in the paragraph by rewriting the entire paragraph.

Assessment: Offer one point for each nonsense word that is replaced by a word or phrase that makes sense.

Paragraph 1:

When I first wake up I throw back the warmerperker and greet the day. I place my feet on the plush furber and feel the softness on my toes. Then I jump up and make my sleepersect. Next I choose coverarms to wear for the day. I get dressed and head downstairs to eat my gerbit with milk. Almost every school day is the same.

Paragraph 2:

I enjoy playing sports. My favorite sport is soccer. I love ramaging up and down the field spurking the ball. In soccer, you cannot touch the ball with your herbits. Sometimes, I am the gulot and get to try to keep the other team from scoring. The gulot is allowed to use their hands to toss the ball back into play. Do you enjoy playing soccer?

Lesson One

Title: We're Going on a Chapter Hunt

Topic: Understanding chapter headings and titles as providing different sections of information

Objective of lesson: Students will locate the chapter that specific information is likely to be in within a text book.

Common Core State Standard used: RL 3.5 Refer to parts of stories, dramas, and poems when writing or speaking about a text, using terms such as chapter, scene, and stanza; describe how each successive part builds on earlier sections.

Materials needed: Textbook for each student (Science or Social Studies is best)

Time for lesson: 15-40 minutes (depending on the number of samples attempted)

Lesson:

- Using the student textbook as an example, show students where to find the table of contents. Explain that the table of contents lists the title of each chapter and the title explains what topic will be explained.

- Offer students an example such as a chapter discussing the Civil War would be in Chapter 3: Wars.

- Allow students to locate chapters with the information you request by using only the titles. Have the chapter number written on a piece of paper.

Assessment: Correct chapter numbers can be used as the assessment.

Lesson Two

Title: I've Scene It

Topic: Understanding scenes in a show and/or book

Objective of lesson: Students will identify the start and end of each scene in a show and book.

Common Core State Standard used: RL 3.5 Refer to parts of stories, dramas, and poems when writing or speaking about a text, using terms such as chapter, scene, and stanza; describe how each successive part builds on earlier sections.

Materials needed: Short video of choice

Text: All of a Kind by Sydney Taylor

Popsicle sticks

Glue

Paper squares

Crayons

Time for lesson: 25-40 minutes (depending on the number of starts and stops as well as video length)

Lesson:

- Explain to students that a scene is somewhat like a new chapter, but can be within a chapter. A new scene starts when the setting changes or other characters take the focus in a discussion all their own.

- Show a short video and at the beginning of each new scene, stop the video to point it out to students.

- Next, have students color a paper square, one side red, and the other green. Glue the popsicle stick to the square.

- Begin reading the chosen text (one is suggested). Each time the scene ends o begins have students hold up the red or green side respectively.

Assessment: Participation and timely responses to the start and end of scenes offers the assessment.

Lesson One

Title: View Finder

Topic: Explaining and comparing different viewpoints

Objective of lesson: Students will compare viewpoints of a single object from different perspectives

Common Core State Standard used: RL 3.6 Distinguish their own point of view from that of the narrator or those of the characters.

Materials needed: Paper

Pencil

Crayons

Desk

3D object that looks different from each side

Time for lesson: 15- 30 minutes (excellent for centers)

Lesson:

- Explain to students that sometimes people view situations differently. Different viewpoints can be informative and offer unique ways to look at things.

- Place students in groups of 3 or 4 and have each at a different angle around a desk with a large object on it. have two students sit and two stand.

- Allow students time to draw the object from their point of view only. Explain that they cannot move or change positions, but must draw what they see only.

- After the drawings are complete, have students compare each viewpoint and discuss the differences with one another.

- Come together as a large group to discuss how perspective can alter people's views. Help students to relate this to reading and character viewpoints.

Assessment: Participation and drawings from appropriate perspectives. You can use art rubric as part of the assessment.

Lesson Two

Title: Rose Colored Glasses

Topic: Explaining and comparing different viewpoints

Objective of lesson: Students will understand different viewpoints through different eyes.

Common Core State Standard used: RL 3.6 Distinguish their own point of view from that of the narrator or those of the characters.

Materials needed:

Colored glasses or colored tissue paper

White objects or white cut out shapes.

Time for lesson: 15-20 minutes (excellent for centers)

Lesson:

- Explain to students that different people view things in different ways. Different viewpoints do not mean that someone is right and someone is wrong, just that things are seen differently.

- Allow students to choose a colored pair of glasses or hold up a piece of colored tissue paper in front of their eyes as you display all white objects.

- The objects will appear to be whatever color tissue paper they are looking through at the time.

- Have students describe what they saw and then view the same object without tissue paper. Which perspective was correct? Both, it was just altered by the paper. Just as perspective can be altered by how you look at things, opinions may change because of those perspectives.

Assessment: Participation and understanding

Lesson One

Title: Colorful Emotions

Topic: Understanding color as a way to elicit emotion

Objective of lesson: Students will learn the meaning of different colors in the use of illustrations.

Common Core State Standard used: RL 3.7 Explain how specific aspects of a text's illustrations contribute to what is conveyed by the words in a story (e.g., create mood, emphasize aspects of a character or setting)

Materials needed: Crayons

Drawing paper

Time for lesson: 25 - 40 minutes (excellent for centers)

Lesson:

- Start as an entire group and discuss such sayings as someone is blue (sad) or someone is green with envy (jealous). Explain to students that some colors are associated with particular feelings.

- Share that authors use these associations to help make people feel a certain way when looking at pictures with text.

- Scribble a dark red blob on a sheet of paper. Ask students what they think of when seeing that (anger, blood, etc.). Explain that red usually represents anger, green jealousy, blue calmness or cold.

- Have students draw a scene using one dominant color and representing a specific emotion. Share the color list (included) to help get them started.

Assessment: Creation of an appropriate drawing, use art rubric for scoring

Color List:

Red – anger

Orange – warmth

Yellow – joy

Green – jealous

Blue – calm or cold

Purple – royal, magical

Black – serious, death

White – pure, clean

Lesson Two

Title: Simple Changes

Topic: Understanding that altering one aspect of a picture or text can alter the meaning and emotion

Objective of lesson: Students will learn that small changes can affect mood and perspective.

Common Core State Standard used: RL 3.7 Explain how specific aspects of a text's illustrations contribute to what is conveyed by the words in a story (e.g., create mood, emphasize aspects of a character or setting)

Materials needed: White, faceless masks

Time for lesson: 15 – 30 minutes

Lesson:

- Explain to students that sometimes we cannot see faces, but we can 'read' body language. Share that often, authors show pictures or describe how a person looks to help us understand how they feel without directly telling us.

- Tell students you are going to give them an example. Put on the white mask and sit up straight and cross your arms as if mad. Tell students to look at you and study your body language.

- Allow students to guess how you were feeling. What led them to their guesses? Try a few more examples.

- Allow students to try to express an emotion with using their face, but just body language.

- Have students work with different partners and continue to do the same.

Assessment: Participation and explanations

Lesson One

Title: Getting Older

Topic: Comparing characters over time

Objective of lesson: Students will compare a character to him/herself as the character ages.

Common Core State Standard used: RL 3.9 Compare and contrast the themes, settings, and plots of stories written by the same author about the same or similar characters (e.g., in books from a series)

Materials needed: Junie B, Jones is a First Grader series book

Junie B. Jones is a Third Grader series book

Time for lesson: 40 - 120 minutes (can be accomplished over several days)

Lesson:

- Have students read or listen to a book out of both series. During reading allow students to take notes on main characters and common behaviors, focusing on how situations are handled.

- After both books in separate series have been read, have students use a Venn diagram to compare a character of their choice from both books.

- After the characters are compared on a Venn have students write a one paragraph summary about the similarities and differences to show how the characters have changed or stayed the same.

Assessment: Accurate summaries of both books, appropriate sentences and appropriate comparisons (see rubric on writing)

Lesson Two

Title: Family Relations

Topic: Comparing two individuals from the same family

Objective of lesson: Students will compare two people from the same family.

Common Core State Standard used: RL 3.9 Compare and contrast the themes, settings, and plots of stories written by the same author about the same or similar characters (e.g., in books from a series)

Materials needed:

Time for lesson: 20 - 40 minutes
Lesson:

- Authors often use the same characters throughout a series of books. Often, even though the characters are from the same town or have the same experiences, they turn into very different types of people. This is also true of family members.

- Have students think about their own siblings or cousins as compared to themselves. Have them list characteristics, physical or otherwise, that are similar and different.

- Have students share the list with a partner. Why are people from the same family so different, but still the same in some ways? Allow students to work with partners or a small group to discuss their reasons. After students share their reasons, explain that it is the same with book characters. Even though characters have the same or similar experiences, personalities can make them handle situations differently. Authors can base their characters on things that could happen in real life or the reactions that may happen in real life.

Assessment: Participation and understanding

Lesson One

Title: Just the Facts

Topic: Writing fact based questions

Objective of lesson: Students will write questions based on a text book topic or chapter.

Common Core State Standard used: RI 3.1 Ask and answer questions to demonstrate understanding of a text, referring explicitly to the text as the basis for the answers.

Materials needed: Textbook

Paper

Pencil

Time for lesson: 30-50 minutes

Lesson:

- Have students read a chapter with partners or in small groups.

- After the chapter is read, have students write three questions based only on the information on the chapter. Make sure the information can be located in the read material.

- Have students choose one question that they feel is the best of the ones they have written. Use everyone's top question to create a test.

- Give the test, but allow students a set amount of time to answer questions using the book. This will reinforce writing factual questions and finding answers in a text book.

Assessment: Give the created test and grade as normal.

Lesson Two

Title: Just the Answers

Topic: Finding factual answers in a text

Objective of lesson: Students will locate the correct answers to questions that are included at the end of textbook chapters.

Common Core State Standard used: RI 3.1 Ask and answer questions to demonstrate understanding of a text, referring explicitly to the text as the basis for the answers.

Materials needed: Textbook

Highlighting tape (per student)

Time for lesson: 30 - 45 minutes

Lesson:

- Have students read a chapter with partners or in small groups.

- After the chapter is read, explain to students that you are going to find the answers to the chapter quiz at the end.

- Read a question to students and ask what the question is actually asking. Have students use the chapter headings to locate the probable place for the answer and find the correct answer.

- Once the answer is located, have students highlight just the answer.

- Repeat for each question.

Assessment: Assessment should be based on the ability to locate relevant information with lessening prompts.

Lesson One

Title: Historical Times

Topic: Recounting key details

Objective of lesson: Students will create a timeline for a historical figure.

Common Core State Standard used: RI 3.2 Determine the main idea of a text; recount the key details and explain how they support the main idea.

Materials needed: Text: Amelia to Zora: Twenty-six Women Who Changed the World by Chin-Lee

Paper

Pencil

Time for lesson: 60 - 80 minutes

Lesson:

- Have students choose a historical figure from the text and read the biography.

- After reading, have students pick out five to ten important events for that particular person.

- Have students order and label these events on a time line and share with at least one partner what the importance of the events are.

Assessment: Assessment should be based on the creation of an accurate times line and the sharing with a partner (see rubric).

Lesson Two

Title: Important Times

Topic: Recounting key details

Objective of lesson: Students will create a timeline for life before and after their birth.

Common Core State Standard used: RI 3.2 Determine the main idea of a text; recount the key details and explain how they support the main idea.

Materials needed: Question sheet (sample included)

Paper

Pencil

Time for lesson: 35 - 45 minutes (plus homework)

Lesson:

- The night before creating the timeline about self, have students take home the question sheet to get help from parents.

- Have students fill in the events of their life on the timeline.

- Remind students that the timeline shows key details of their life and what has been important leading up to their birth. This is much like the opening of a book or story when background information on each character is given.

- Have students draw an illustration to accompany the life timeline. *If it helps, have students label timelines BM-before me or AM- after me*

Assessment: Assessment should be based on the creation of an accurate times line and the gathering of information.

Sample Information (for timeline homework)

Parent's birthdays

Sibling's birthdays

At least three important events in the student's life with dates

At least three important events prior to student's birth with dates

Lesson One

Title: Order Up

Topic: Sequencing

Objective of lesson: Students will place pictures and descriptions in sequential order.

Common Core State Standard used: RI 3.3 Describe the relationship between a series of historical events, scientific ideas or concepts, or steps in technical procedures in a text, using language that pertains to time, sequence, and cause/effect.

Materials needed: Science text(s)

Paper

Markers/pencils

Scissors

Writing pencil

Time for lesson: 40 - 60 minutes

Lesson:

- Allow students to choose one of the following science topics (water cycle, animal food chain, respiration of a human, or photosynthesis)

- Have students illustrate the cycle with both pictures and in writing.

- Have students cut out each picture and information (sample shown)

- Next students are to find a partner that chose a cycle different than their own.

- Have the partner piece the cycle back together in sequential order.

Assessment: Assessment should be based on the creation of an accurate cycle and reconstruction.

Sample;

Picture	
Description	

Picture	
Description	

Picture	
Description	

Picture	
Description	

Picture	
Description	

Lesson Two

Title: How-To

Topic: Sequencing

Objective of lesson: Students will create a step by step manual for a common task, with illustrations.

Common Core State Standard used: RI 3.3 Describe the relationship between a series of historical events, scientific ideas or concepts, or steps in technical procedures in a text, using language that pertains to time, sequence, and cause/effect.

Materials needed:

Paper (several sheets per student, folded in half plus a cover)

Markers/pencils

Writing pencil

Time for lesson: 45 - 60 minutes

Lesson:

- Allow students to choose one of the following skills (brushing your teeth, washing your hair, making a bed, making a sandwich)

- Have students create a How-to manual with written directions and illustrations on the chosen skill. Remind students that people cannot do anything they are not told to by the manual so be very specific.

- Have students follow their own directions to see if the skills are appropriate.

- After they have been written, chose a couple that wrote about the sandwich and have them read it as you do everything they say. Make sure to over exaggerate any step that doesn't make sense.

Assessment: Assessment should be based on the creation of an accurate manual and appropriate writing as based on the writing rubric.

Lesson One

Title: Dictionary Dash

Topic: Determining the meanings of words

Objective of lesson: Students will use a dictionary or glossary to define specific terms.

Common Core State Standard used: RI 3.4 Determine the meaning of general academic and domain-specific words and phrases in a text relevant to a *grade 3 topic or subject area.*

Materials needed:

Dictionary or text with glossary

Subject specific word list

Time for lesson: 10 - 25 minutes (small groups if dictionary skills are lacking)

Lesson:

- Have a list of subject specific words for the text or topic you are using.

- Tell students to find the glossary section and give them the beginning letter for the next word.

- Tell students the goal is to find the word the fastest and raise their hand as soon as it is found.

- Read the word and allow students to search. Choose someone with their hand raised to read the definition. Offer that student a sticker or other small object. *This is a great way to build dictionary skills and keep students busy while waiting for lunch or bus time.

Assessment: Assessment should be based on appropriate use of a dictionary or glossary.

Lesson Two

Title: Tear It Up

Topic: Understanding grade appropriate terms

Objective of lesson: Students will define grade specific terms and play a game to learn other grade appropriate terminology.

Common Core State Standard used: RI 3.4 Determine the meaning of general academic and domain-specific words and phrases in a text relevant to a *grade 3 topic or subject area.*

Materials needed: Pencils

Dictionary or text with glossary

Subject specific word list

Colored paper strips

Scissors

Time for lesson: 30 -60 minutes

Lesson:

- Have a list of words appropriate for the lesson written on the board.

- Separate students into groups of three or four and give each student in the group the same color strip of paper. Each group should have a different color.

- Tell students to fold the paper into three squares and choose one word from the list. In the first square write the chosen word (each group member should have a different word). Second square, write a short definition. Third square should include a picture to illustrate the word or concept.

- Have students cut apart the squares and mix them up with the other members of the group. Have groups exchange pieces of paper.

- When you say go, see which teams can work together to correctly piece the strips together. This is a great way to practice vocabulary and prepare for tests.

- If time allows have student more groups and repeat.

Assessment: Assessment should be based on correctly reassembling strips of paper.

Lesson One

Title: Wanted for Being Famous

Topic: Using online resources

Objective of lesson: Students will use Google images and a generic search to learn about historical figures

Common Core State Standard used: RI 3.5 Use text features and search tools (e.g., key words, sidebars, hyperlinks) to locate information relevant to a given topic efficiently.

Materials needed: Poster paper

Markers/colored pencils

Computers with Internet access

Printer

Glue

Time for lesson: 45 - 60 minutes

Lesson:

- Give students a list of famous people to choose from or assign specific historical figures.

- Explain to students how to complete an Internet search for information on the figure and how to determine a site that offers accurate information. Make sure that you have reviewed internet safety with the students.

- Have students search for information on their given figures and record at least 5 facts from different sites.

- Next have students find a photo, using Google images, of their figure. Print the photo or drawing.

- Have students create a 'Wanted' poster for their historical figure that includes the photo or drawing and a list of facts about the figure.

Assessment: Assessment should be based on correctly using the Internet and creation of poster. (See rubric about brochure)

Lesson Two

Title: Online Museum

Topic: Using online resources

Objective of lesson: Students will use an online museum to gather information.

Common Core State Standard used: RI 3.5 Use text features and search tools (e.g., key words, sidebars, hyperlinks) to locate information relevant to a given topic efficiently.

Materials needed: Pencil

Paper (or question sheet if using a specific section) teacher created

Computers with Internet access

Time for lesson: 40 - 50 minutes

Lesson:

- Explain to students that sometimes travelling to a museum is not possible, but we can use online tools, such as digital museums to learn about different topics.

- Help students navigate to http://airandspace.si.edu/education/onlinelearning.cfm

- Choose an area for study or to answer questions for students to explore.

- Offer students the question list that has been created ahead of time.

- Allow students time to answer questions and explore the online museum.

Assessment: Assessment should be based on correctly using the internet and correct answers to questions.

Lesson One

Title: Slave Labor

Topic: Learning to distinguish perspective.

Objective of lesson: Students will distinguish their point of view from that of others.

Common Core State Standard used: RI 3.6 Distinguish their own point of view from that of the author of a text.

Materials needed: Text: ...If You Lived When There Was Slavery in America by A. Kamma

Paper

Pencil

Time for lesson: 2 days

Lesson:

- Inform parents of this activity before beginning

- Split students into pairs, explain that the first day half of the students will have to listen to their partner, and then they will switch places.

- The 'slave' for the day will get paper and other supplies for students, should get the partners lunch tray, and will be asked to play indoors while the others go outside for recess. A special activity may also require 'slaves' to sit in less preferential seating.

- Roles will reverse the next day.

- At the end of the second day have students write about their experiences in both positions. Explain that people used to actually work as slaves and often conditions were far from desirable, but these people did not have a choice.

- Discuss that this activity – slavery – has happened all over the world. If there is a certain topic that relates to what you will be teaching that year, explain how it ties into what they have been doing for this time period.

- Share the text to offer perspective and bring the lesson together.

Assessment: Assessment should be based on writing rubric.

Lesson Two

Title: Tell Me About It

Topic: Learning to distinguish perspective

Objective of lesson: Students will distinguish different viewpoints

Common Core State Standard used: RI 3.6 Distinguish their own point of view from that of the author of a text.

Materials needed: Text: The American Story: 100 True Tales from American History by Armstrong

Paper

Pencil

Time for lesson: 45 - 60 minutes

Lesson:

- This lesson can be used over and over with different tales. It can also be adapted to a discussion group or writing assignment.

- Read a story from the text to all students. Starting with the Wright brother's story is recommended. Have students explain how the Wright brothers felt about their goal of a 'flying machine'. Now ask students to think about others who were hearing about what the brothers were doing. How must outsiders have felt? What did they think?

- Share another story from the book and ask students to take a perspective from someone outside the actual event.

- Have students compose a letter to a friend about what is happening and the feelings that it creates.

Assessment: Assessment should be based on writing rubric.

Lesson One

Title: Key Words Only

Topic: Understanding text

Objective of lesson: Students will show understanding of a text through key word identification.

Common Core State Standard used: RI 3.7 Use information gained from illustrations (e.g., maps, photographs) and the words in a text to demonstrate understanding of the text (e.g., where, when, why, and how key events occur).

Materials needed: Text: Any informational text with photos or accurate drawings

Pencil

ABC chart

Time for lesson: 40 -60 minutes

Lesson:

- Allow students to read or listen to the chosen text

- Hand out individual copies of the ABC chart (included)

- Explain to students that the alpha-boxes are going to offer a summary for others who have not read what they have read.

- Each box should have one or two words that begin with that letter that are key words in the reading or describe the main topic and details.

Assessment: Assessment should be based on appropriate word choices.

A	B	C	D
E	F	G	H
I	JK	L	M
N	O	P	QR
S	T	U	V
W	XYZ		

Lesson Two

Title: Five W's

Topic: Understanding text

Objective of lesson: Students will show understanding of a text through the answering of who, what, where, when, and why.

Common Core State Standard used: RI 3.7 Use information gained from illustrations (e.g., maps, photographs) and the words in a text to demonstrate understanding of the text (e.g., where, when, why, and how key events occur).

Materials needed: Text: The American Story: 100 True Tales from American History by Armstrong

Dry erase markers

Paper in sheet protector (serves as a dry erase board)

Time for lesson: 20 - 30 minutes (per group)

Lesson:

- Have students write the 5 W's (who, what, when, where, and why) on their personal dry erase boards.

- As a story from the text is shared have students pick out and write the information from the passage that answers each question.

- All answers should be completed during reading. Choose a different story for each group.

- Time permitting, allow groups to come together to share what has been learned.

Assessment: Assessment should be based on appropriate answers.

Lesson One

Title: That Sentence Shows….

Topic: Distinguishing sentence types

Objective of lesson: Students will identify sentence types, including comparison, cause/effect, and sequencing.

Common Core State Standard used: RI 3.8 Describe the logical connection between particular sentences and paragraphs in a text (e.g., comparison, cause/effect, first/second/third in a sequence).

Materials needed: Worksheet (included)

Time for lesson: 20 - 30 minutes

Lesson:

- Before handing out the worksheet, explain the differences in the types of sentences. Cause and effect means that one thing caused another and often uses the words if/then. Sequencing is a series of steps or ordered events. Comparison sentences are showing the similarities and/or differences of two or more objects.

- Tell students to label the provided sentences as comparison, cause/effect, or sequencing.

Assessment: Assessment should be based on correct answers (included).

Sample Worksheet:

Label the following sentences as either comparison, cause/effect, or sequencing.

1. When the sun gets hot, ice cream melts.

2. If I pour water on a young plant, then it should grow larger.

3. The sun is bright orange just like my basketball.

4. First we are going to the airport, then flying to California, and finally we will see my grandparents.

5. The photo looked like a painting.

6. Move the bed out from the wall then put the sheet on.

Write and label an example of each sentence type.

7.

_____

_____

8.

_____

_____

9.

_____

_____

Answer Sheet

1. Cause/effect

2. Cause/effect

3. Comparison

4. Sequence

5. Comparison

6. Sequence

Lesson Two

Title: Cause That Effect

Topic: Distinguishing cause and effect

Objective of lesson: Students will identify the cause and effect in a sentence.

Common Core State Standard used: RI 3.8 Describe the logical connection between particular sentences and paragraphs in a text (e.g., comparison, cause/effect, first/second/third in a sequence).

Materials needed: Worksheet (included)

Highlighters (2 colors per child)

Time for lesson: 25 - 40 minutes (This lesson is perfect for a white board if one is available)

Lesson:

- Project the included sentences on the whiteboard or offer each child their own sheet.

- Explain that each sentence has a cause and effect included and the cause will be highlighted in one color with the effect in a different color.

- Allow children to take turns marking sentences or have all finish the worksheet.

Assessment: Assessment should be based on correct answers (included).

1. The sun warms the plant allowing it to grow.

2. The car moves forward when I push on the gas.

3. Pushing the button turns on the light.

4. Watching too much television has harmed my eyesight.

5. Mom is happy when I clean my room.

6. The teacher yells less when we behave.

7. We behave when the teacher does not give much work.

8. When lunch is late I get hungry.

9. I eat cereal when mom does not cook.

10. I won the contest because I worked hard on my project.

Answer Sheet

Cause   Effect

1. The sun warms the plant allowing it to grow.

2. The car moves forward when I push on the gas.

3. Pushing the button turns on the light.

4. Watching too much television has harmed my eyesight.

5. Mom is happy when I clean my room.

6. The teacher yells less when we behave.

7. We behave when the teacher does not give much work.

8. When lunch is late I get hungry.

9. I eat cereal when mom does not cook.

10. I won the contest because I worked hard on my project.

Lesson One

Title: Compare It

Topic: Comparing books on similar topics

Objective of lesson: Students will use two different books on the same topic to compare information.

Common Core State Standard used: RI 3.9 Compare and contrast the most important points and key details presented in two texts on the same topic.

Materials needed: Text: Go Free or Die, A Story about Harriet Tubman by Ferris and Harriet Tubman by Gresko (recommended)

Time for lesson: 45 - 60 minutes

Lesson:

- Have students read or listen to both texts on Harriet Tubman.

- Have small groups of children create a chart or other visual of their choosing to compare the information in both texts. Have students search for small discrepancies such as dates of death or place of birth.

- As a large group discuss the findings and have students hypothesize on why some 'factual' information may vary.

Assessment: Assessment should be based on fact finding and discussion participation.

Lesson Two

Title: Debate It

Topic: Discussing facts on both sides of an issue

Objective of lesson: Students will debate on teams

Common Core State Standard used: RI 3.9 Compare and contrast the most important points and key details presented in two texts on the same topic.

Materials needed: Computer with Internet access

Time for lesson: 45 - 60 minutes

Lesson:

- Choose an appropriate topic for your class. This could range from a political debate to the choice of food in the lunch room.

- Explain to students that most issues have two sides, neither is good or bad, but there are always two viewpoints.

- Split the class and give each team an issue to debate.

- Have students research their topic and tell them they need to be prepared to debate the topic.

- Explain that everyone in the group must participate and say at least one thing during the debate.

- Allow students to debate the topic.

Assessment: Assessment should be based on fact finding and discussion participation.

Lesson One

Title: Talk to Me

Topic: Phonetic practice

Objective of lesson: Students will practice saying multi-syllable words with a partner.

- Common Core State Standard used: RF 3.3 Know and apply grade-level phonics and word analysis skills in decoding words.

  - CCSS.ELA-Literacy.RF.3.3a Identify and know the meaning of the most common prefixes and derivational suffixes.

  - CCSS.ELA-Literacy.RF.3.3b Decode words with common Latin suffixes.

  - CCSS.ELA-Literacy.RF.3.3c Decode multi-syllable words.

  - CCSS.ELA-Literacy.RF.3.3d Read grade-appropriate irregularly spelled words.

Materials needed: List of multisyllabic words (included)

Timer

Checklist

Time for lesson: 5-10 minutes

Lesson:

- Have students pair off, groups of two or three are appropriate)

- Set the timer for 1 minutes/30 seconds if strong readers

- Have students read off as many multi-syllabic words as possible in the 1 minute.

- Record the number of correctly read words as marked by the partner

- Repeat as desired to increase fluency of multisyllabic words. *Great as a morning warm-up.

Assessment: Assessment should be based on increased fluency over time.

Starter List

bedroom	bathroom	campground	playroom
birdhouse	backfire	sandpaper	snowman
butterfly	candlestick	daylight	nightgown
homesick	homeroom	footprint	footman
football	anytime	anyone	everything
raincoat	sunset	anywhere	everyone
rainfall	waterfall	something	everywhere
doghouse	someone	background	somewhere

Lesson Two

Title: Match Maker

Topic: Practice with common prefixes

Objective of lesson: Students will practice matching prefixes to meanings.

- Common Core State Standard used: RF 3.3 Know and apply grade-level phonics and word analysis skills in decoding words.

    - CCSS.ELA-Literacy.RF.3.3a Identify and know the meaning of the most common prefixes and derivational suffixes.

    - CCSS.ELA-Literacy.RF.3.3b Decode words with common Latin suffixes.

    - CCSS.ELA-Literacy.RF.3.3c Decode multi-syllable words.

    - CCSS.ELA-Literacy.RF.3.3d Read grade-appropriate irregularly spelled words.

Materials needed: List of prefixes and meanings (included)

Scissors

Time for lesson: 5 minutes

Lesson:

- Have students cut apart the list of common prefixes and meanings after studying the sheet. If you can laminate the sheets before cutting, tiles can be reused.

- Set a timer and have students match prefixes to meaning.

- Alternate method is to pair students and turn all tiles face down after cutting apart. Play a memory matching game in which two tiles are turned over and if they match, the pair is kept, if not the next person goes until all tiles have been matched.

Assessment: Assessment should be based on appropriate matching within the time limit.

Study List

dis – not, do the opposite of, exclude

con- together with, jointly

non- no, not, without

ex- from, out, away from

re- again, back

mis- bad, badly, wrong

un-not, opposite of, lacking

pre- earlier, before

Tiles (to be cut)

dis	not, do opposite of, exclude
non	no, not, without
re	again, back
un	not, opposite of, lacking
con	together with, jointly
ex	from, out, away from
mis	bad, badly, wrong
pre	earlier, before

Lesson One

Title: Reader's Choice

Topic: Practice with reading aloud

Objective of lesson: Students will practice reading to others

Common Core State Standard used: RF 3.4 Read with sufficient accuracy and fluency to support comprehension.

- CCSS.ELA-Literacy.RF.3.4a Read grade-level text with purpose and understanding.

- CCSS.ELA-Literacy.RF.3.4b Read grade-level prose and poetry orally with accuracy, appropriate rate, and expression.

- CCSS.ELA-Literacy.RF.3.4c Use context to confirm or self-correct word recognition and understanding, rereading as necessary.

Materials needed: Access to library

Time for lesson: 15 - 30 minutes daily

Lesson:

- Allow students to visit the library weekly or offer a range of books within the classroom. Each day (tell children ahead of time) have one or two children share a book or poem that they enjoy. The book should be short enough to be shared in 10-20 minutes.

- Model good listening skills and a supportive environment for students who are reading and listening.

Assessment: Assessment should be based on reading aloud.

Lesson Two

Title: Listen to Me

Topic: Practice reading aloud and self correcting

Objective of lesson: Students will practice reading and recording and then improving reading skills.

Common Core State Standard used: RF 3.4 Read with sufficient accuracy and fluency to support comprehension.

- CCSS.ELA-Literacy.RF.3.4a Read grade-level text with purpose and understanding.

- CCSS.ELA-Literacy.RF.3.4b Read grade-level prose and poetry orally with accuracy, appropriate rate, and expression.

- CCSS.ELA-Literacy.RF.3.4c Use context to confirm or self-correct word recognition and understanding, rereading as necessary.

Materials needed: Access to computers with internet

Student chosen text

Time for lesson: 15 - 30 minutes

Lesson:

- Make sure computers have microphones, speakers, and headphones, as well as the free program Audacity for the computer http://audacity.sourceforge.net/

- Have students choose a favorite book, poem, chapter to record themselves reading.

- After recording, have students listen to the recording and critique their style.

- Have students practice different text types over time to increase fluency

- Assessment: Assessment should be based on reading aloud and properly using the computer.

Lesson One

Title: Opinions About it All

Topic: Writing opinion pieces

Objective of lesson: Students will write an opinion piece on a school related topic

- Common Core State Standard used: W 3.1 Write opinion pieces on topics or texts, supporting a point of view with reasons.

  - CCSS.ELA-Literacy.W.3.1a Introduce the topic or text they are writing about, state an opinion, and create an organizational structure that lists reasons.

  - CCSS.ELA-Literacy.W.3.1b Provide reasons that support the opinion.

  - CCSS.ELA-Literacy.W.3.1c Use linking words and phrases (e.g., *because, therefore, since, for example*) to connect opinion and reasons.

  - CCSS.ELA-Literacy.W.3.1d Provide a concluding statement or section.

Materials needed: Paper or computer

Pencil

Time for lesson: 30-60 minutes

Lesson:

- Offer students a list of school related topics.

- Explain that sometimes an opinion is expected in writing, but that writing should be backed up with logical reasoning or facts.

- Have students write an opinion piece, with facts or strong reasoning about a chosen topic. Explain the rubric to students before writing is graded so corrections can be made as needed.

Assessment: Assessment should be based on writing rubric.

Possible Topics

Quality of school lunches

Homework: Good or bad

Physical education: Good or bad

Recess: To short or good length

School start time: To early or just right

Lesson Two

Title: Before And After

Topic: Opinion writing

Objective of lesson: Students will write an opinion piece.

- Common Core State Standard used: W 3.1 Write opinion pieces on topics or texts, supporting a point of view with reasons.

  - CCSS.ELA-Literacy.W.3.1a Introduce the topic or text they are writing about, state an opinion, and create an organizational structure that lists reasons.

  - CCSS.ELA-Literacy.W.3.1b Provide reasons that support the opinion.

  - CCSS.ELA-Literacy.W.3.1c Use linking words and phrases (e.g., *because, therefore, since, for example*) to connect opinion and reasons.

  - CCSS.ELA-Literacy.W.3.1d Provide a concluding statement or section.

Materials needed: Paper or computer

Pencil

Time for lesson: 30-60 minutes (before and after event)

Lesson:

- Talk to students about an upcoming school or national event that they can either attend of watch on television.

- Have students write about what they think the event will be like, what can be expected, and any other opinions they may have on the activity.

- After attending or watching the event, have students write opinions about what has happened or how it was different than expected.

- Have a class discussion about the differences in expectations and actual events and how opinions can change over time and experience.

Assessment: Assessment should be based on writing rubric.

Lesson One

Title: Let Me Check My Schedule

Topic: Clearly presenting information

Objective of lesson: Students will clearly inform the reader of a typical day.

- Common Core State Standard used: W 3.2 Write informative/explanatory texts to examine a topic and convey ideas and information clearly.

  o CCSS.ELA-Literacy.W.3.2a Introduce a topic and group related information together; include illustrations when useful to aiding comprehension.

  o CCSS.ELA-Literacy.W.3.2b Develop the topic with facts, definitions, and details.

  o CCSS.ELA-Literacy.W.3.2c Use linking words and phrases (e.g., *also, another, and, more,but*) to connect ideas within categories of information.

  o CCSS.ELA-Literacy.W.3.2d Provide a concluding statement or section.

Materials needed: Paper or computer

Pencil

Time for lesson: 20-30 minutes

Lesson:

- Explain to students that we must be very detailed in writing when specifics need to be shared. One way to practice sharing specifics for a day is by making a schedule.

- Have students write a schedule for their typical school day. Include times, activities, and a place to mark off a finished activity.

- Allow students to attempt to keep the schedule both during and after school for a day or two.

Assessment: Assessment should be based on creating a logical schedule.

Lesson Two

Title: Put it in Your Own Words

Topic: Sharing an idea clearly

Objective of lesson: Students will use directions for a task and rewrite so those directions are in simple language.

- Common Core State Standard used: W 3.2 Write informative/explanatory texts to examine a topic and convey ideas and information clearly.

    - CCSS.ELA-Literacy.W.3.2a Introduce a topic and group related information together; include illustrations when useful to aiding comprehension.

    - CCSS.ELA-Literacy.W.3.2b Develop the topic with facts, definitions, and details.

    - CCSS.ELA-Literacy.W.3.2c Use linking words and phrases (e.g., *also, another, and, more, but*) to connect ideas within categories of information.

    - CCSS.ELA-Literacy.W.3.2d Provide a concluding statement or section.

Materials needed: Paper or computer

Pencil

Time for lesson: 45 - 60 minutes

Lesson:

- Allow students to choose a task that they are familiar with. This can be something such as building a tower or brushing their teeth.

- Allow students to write a detailed description of their chosen task. It works well when they explain a skill related to a hobby, such as how to kick a soccer ball or shoot a basket.

- Allow class members to attempt to follow directions as written and learn new skills

Assessment: Assessment should be based on logical and sequential directions.

Lesson One

Title: I Spy

Topic: Using descriptive writing

Objective of lesson: Students will use descriptive writing to describe an unnamed object.

- Common Core State Standard used: W 3.3 Write narratives to develop real or imagined experiences or events using effective technique, descriptive details, and clear event sequences.

  - CCSS.ELA-Literacy.W.3.3a Establish a situation and introduce a narrator and/or characters; organize an event sequence that unfolds naturally.

  - CCSS.ELA-Literacy.W.3.3b Use dialogue and descriptions of actions, thoughts, and feelings to develop experiences and events or show the response of characters to situations.

  - CCSS.ELA-Literacy.W.3.3c Use temporal words and phrases to signal event order.

  - CCSS.ELA-Literacy.W.3.3d Provide a sense of closure.

Materials needed: Paper or computer

Pencil

Time for lesson: 20 - 60 minutes

Lesson:

- Allow students to choose an object from the classroom, but do not allow them to tell others what the object is, just an object they can easily see.

- Have students write a description of the object without ever naming it directly.

- Share descriptions and allow other students to guess what the described object could be.

Assessment: Assessment should be based on the writing rubric.

Sample: Pencil

The main, long cylindrical base is used for holding. One end holds a light pink rubber tip that can remove some mistakes. The other end is often sharp, but can be made dull with time and use. The base is goldenrod in color, but wooden underneath. What is being described?

Lesson Two

Title: And.....Scene

Topic: Using descriptive writing to create a scene

Objective of lesson: Students will use descriptive writing to describe an event which is then acted out.

- Common Core State Standard used: W 3.3 Write narratives to develop real or imagined experiences or events using effective technique, descriptive details, and clear event sequences.

    o CCSS.ELA-Literacy.W.3.3a Establish a situation and introduce a narrator and/or characters; organize an event sequence that unfolds naturally.

    o CCSS.ELA-Literacy.W.3.3b Use dialogue and descriptions of actions, thoughts, and feelings to develop experiences and events or show the response of characters to situations.

    o CCSS.ELA-Literacy.W.3.3c Use temporal words and phrases to signal event order.

    o CCSS.ELA-Literacy.W.3.3d Provide a sense of closure.

Materials needed: Paper or computer

Pencil

Time for lesson: 30-90 minutes

Lesson:

- Split students into groups of 3 or 4. Explain that the students must agree on an activity that they will act out and describe without ever naming the activity.

- Each person must have at least one line or action in the skit for credit.

- Have students first write a few lines for the skit, then practice, and act out the skit for the class. Video students if possible so they may watch themselves later.

- Have those not in the skit guess what is being acted out and described in the skit.

Assessment: Assessment should be based on participation and working with a group rubric.

Sample: "Wow look at how high that is!"

"Oh no! I'm a little scared."

"Me too, but I love going fast so it should be fun."

"Look! There goes a group of people. Look how high the first hill is."

"I will probably scream the entire time."

"Do you put your arms up going down hills?"

"We are next, let's go."

(What is it? Roller coaster ride)

Lesson One

Title: My Hobby

Topic: Practice writing and editing with guidance

Objective of lesson: Students will create a writing piece that is then edited and rewritten with suggestions in place.

Common Core State Standard used: W 3.5 With guidance and support from peers and adults, develop and strengthen writing as needed by planning, revising, and editing.

Materials needed: Paper

Pencil

Colored pencils

Time for lesson: 30-90 minutes (may take more than one day depending on story length)

Lesson:

- Have students decide on a hobby that they wish to share about with the class. Explain that the first step to writing is planning and have students write the name of the hobby and 5-7 points that they wish to discuss in their writing.

- Using that list of points, have students come up with an opening to the writing that will introduce the topic smoothly. (i.e. Many people have hobbies, my favorite hobby is…).

- Have students exchange opening lines and allow at least two other students to comment about the opener or make necessary changes.

- Have students begin writing their piece based on the created list and edited opening.

- After writing have students trade stories with at least two other students and offer suggestions and edits.

- Allow the author to utilize the edits and create a final (typed if possible) copy for grading.

Assessment: Assessment should be based on writing/editing rubric.

Lesson Two

Title: Computer Based Editing

Topic: Practice writing and editing with guidance

Objective of lesson: Students will create a writing piece that is then edited and rewritten with suggestions in place.

Common Core State Standard used: W 3.5 With guidance and support from peers and adults, develop and strengthen writing as needed by planning, revising, and editing.

Materials needed: Computer with Word (or similar program with track changes)

Time for lesson: 30 - 90 minutes (may take more than one day depending on story length)

Lesson:

- Have students decide on a topic that they wish to share about with the class.

- Allow students to create a story or writing piece of your choice.

- After writing is complete allow students to exchange files and use the 'track changes' option to edit another student's paper.

- Allow the original student to accept or deny any suggested changes, including spelling corrections.

- Allow students to add clip art or a photo and print for display.

Assessment: Assessment should be based on writing/editing rubric.

Lesson One

Title: Technology Tell All

Topic: Practice using technology to illustrate writing

Objective of lesson: Students will create a computer generated brochure about themselves, including clip art or photos.

Common Core State Standard used: W 3.6 With guidance and support from adults, use technology to produce and publish writing (using keyboarding skills) as well as to interact and collaborate with others.

Materials needed: Computer with Publisher (or similar program)

Time for lesson: 30-90 minutes

Lesson:

- Have students bring in pictures to scan or flash drives with appropriate photos prior to assignment.

- Teach students to open a brochure or publishing file.

- Brochures should include at least two photos or pieces of clip art and 5 different aspects of the student's life (family, hobbies, pets, friends, favorites, etc)

Assessment: Assessment should be based on brochure making rubric.

Lesson Two

Title: Technological Feedback

Topic: Practice using technology to create writing

Objective of lesson: Students will create a writing piece on the computer.

Common Core State Standard used: W 3.6 With guidance and support from adults, use technology to produce and publish writing (using keyboarding skills) as well as to interact and collaborate with others.

Materials needed: Computer with Internet access

Time for lesson: 30 minutes

Lesson:

- Help students navigate to http://www.funenglishgames.com/writinggames/story.html

- Allow students to choose the type of story that they would like to create. The program will give them words to choose from to make a story have the right type of setting and scene. After students practice with at least two story types, help them open a free writing program of choice.

- Have students create their own original setting for a story using appropriate word choices. (About 1 paragraph)

Assessment: Assessment should be based on participation with the program, appropriate computer use, and a logical paragraph with appropriate wording.

Lesson One

Title: Library Look-Up

Topic: Learning to research a topic

Objective of lesson: Students will use the computerized library catalog to locate books for research before creating a short report.

Common Core State Standard used: W 3.7 Conduct short research projects that build knowledge about a topic.

Materials needed: Computer

Library

Paper

Pencil

Time for lesson: 1 week (30-60 minute sessions)

Lesson:

- Offer students a list of topics to choose from or allow students to choose a topic for research. Explain that though most research is now found online, the students will first use books as a basis for information.

- Allow students to visit the library and locate at least two books on the given topic. These two books will be basis for a mini-research paper.

- Teach students how to do basic in text references (Author, date).

- Allow students time to read the books and write a paper with sections such as characteristics, historical facts, and current population. Also make sure students use an introduction and closing.

- Time permitting, allow students to create a cover for their individual report.

Assessment: Assessment should be based on basic writing rubric.

Lesson Two

Title: Online Scavenger Hunt

Topic: Learning to find answers using a computer

Objective of lesson: Students will use the computer to answer provided questions on a given topic.

Common Core State Standard used: W 3.7 Conduct short research projects that build knowledge about a topic.

Materials needed: Computer with Internet access

List of sites (included)

Question sheets (included)

Time for lesson: 30-45 minutes

Lesson:*If websites are difficult for students to type, try using tiny url to shorten it.

- Offer students a list of websites and the question sheet. Explain that they will do an online scavenger hunt to answer each question.

- Explain to students that not all information can always be found in one place and that we should always find at least two reliable sources that have the same information.

- As students find answers have them write out which website the information was found on.

Assessment: Assessment should be based on finding correct answers and listing correct websites.

Website list:

1. http://pbskids.org/eekoworld/

2. http://www.earthmatters4kids.org/main.html

3. http://amazing-space.stsci.edu/

1. What are three animals found in deciduous forests? (Hint look under the environment tab)

2. Where does the water cycle start? (Hint try the living lab for students)

3. How might the beach look different in the future if people do not care for the environment? List at least three changes. (Hint look into the future)

4. Go to the site that allows you to explore Mars. Find the link in which you can ask Dr. C a question. Write the question you ask and the response given. (Hint Mars Fun Zone, start exploring)

5. What do the cameras on the Rover's head photograph? (Hint Mar's Science Laboratory)

6. If the Rover was human, about how tall would it be?

7. What three types of antennae can be found on the Rover?

Challenge: Create your own Eekocreature. Draw what you created here.

Answers: 1) deer, squirrels, beaver

2) lakes, oceans, rivers

3) trash in the water, insects, dead fish, smelly

4) Answers will vary

5) landscapes

6) 7 feet tall

7) UHF, high gain, and low gain

Lesson One

Title: Sort it Out .com

Topic: Categorization of websites

Objective of lesson: Students will practice separating websites into categories.

Common Core State Standard used: W 3.8 Recall information from experiences or gather information from print and digital sources; take brief notes on sources and sort evidence into provided categories.

Materials needed: Computer with internet access

List of sites (included)

Time for lesson: 30-45 minutes

Lesson:

- Explain to students that we use the internet for many different types of jobs. Sometimes we research for school projects, sometimes we may shop online, and sometimes we may want to listen to music.

- Explain that some sites provide this different information and are more reliable than others. Websites that end in .edu are educational, .gov are created and maintained by government agencies, and .com can be anyone so the sources may be reliable or not.

- Provide students with a list of websites to visit and have them determine which category the site would fall into.

Assessment: Assessment should be based on correctly organizing sites based on given criteria.

Educational	Government Run	Shopping	Entertainment	Informational, Not always reliable

List of sites: *Print sites on sticky paper and have categories on the board so students can place them if working in small groups.

Sites:

1. www.wikipedia.com

2. www.youtube.com

3. www.funbrain.com

4. http://kids.nationalgeographic.com/kids/

5. http://www.poptropica.com/

6. www.walmart.com

7. www.facebook.com

8. http://www.kidzone.ws/

9. www.usa.gov

10. http://kids.usa.gov/government/index.shtml

Lesson Two

Title: Tell Me More...

Topic: Gathering information

Objective of lesson: Students will interview a partner to gather and write up information.

Common Core State Standard used: W 3.8 Recall information from experiences or gather information from print and digital sources; take brief notes on sources and sort evidence into provided categories.

Materials needed: Paper

Pencil

Time for lesson: 60 - 90 minutes – can be done over several days

Lesson:

- Tell students that they are going to be reporters for the day. Explain that they will interview people in the school (or in the classroom) and then share what they have learned with the class or a small group.

- If interviews are to be set up with others in the school (principal, janitor, secretary, lunch lady, etc) then contact these individuals ahead of time and allow the students to ask for an interview and an appropriate time. Otherwise, students can interview one another or family members.

- Have students work together to come up with at least 5 questions that are appropriate for the person being interviewed. Review questions before allowing interviews.

- Allow students to interview and record answers. Remind students that they do not have to write word for word but should note enough to remember what was said.

- After interviews have students create a news-type article about the person interviewed. Include a photo or drawing if possible.

Assessment: Assessment should be based on using appropriate interviewing techniques (see rubric).

Lesson One

Title: Today I Feel

Topic: Free writing

Objective of lesson: Students will practice short stints of daily writing.

Common Core State Standard used: W 3.10 Write routinely over extended time frames (time for research, reflection, and revision) and shorter time frames (a single sitting or a day or two) for a range of discipline-specific tasks, purposes, and audiences.

Materials needed: Journal

Pencil

Timer

Time for lesson: 5 minutes (per day)

Lesson:

- Each morning have students get out an individualized journal.

- Set the timer for five minutes. Explain to students that what they write about is not as important as the fact they are writing for the entire time, but each entry should begin with Today I feel….

- Journals are to remain private unless they student chooses to share, but the teacher will review as needed to assess writing.

Assessment: Assessment should be based on the improvement of writing in length, word choice, and spelling over time.

Lesson Two

Title: Pass it On

Topic: Group Writing

Objective of lesson: Students will practice adding to stories

Common Core State Standard used: W 3.10 Write routinely over extended time frames (time for research, reflection, and revision) and shorter time frames (a single sitting or a day or two) for a range of discipline-specific tasks, purposes, and audiences.

Materials needed: Paper

Pencil

Time for lesson: 10-30 minutes

Lesson:

- Tell students they are going to be story tellers, but they are going to tell a story at the same time. (25 –number of students)

- Explain that students will write each story one sentence at a time. Each will start their own story in any way they wish. (Once upon a time a prince was in love with a princess or The scary monster waited under the bed for the man to come home, etc)

- After writing the first sentence the paper should be passed to the next writer to add one sentence. This should continue until everyone has added one sentence to each paper. At the end the authors should get their paper back to write an ending based on what has been added.

- Share stories with the class if time permits.

Assessment: Assessment should be based on adding appropriate sentences and participation.

Lesson One

Title: Tiny Teachers

Topic: Presenting information with a group

Objective of lesson: Students will present information in a given chapter to the class as a whole.

Common Core State Standard used: SL 3.1 Engage effectively in a range of collaborative discussions (one-on-one, in groups, and teacher-led) with diverse partners on *grade 3 topics and texts*, building on others' ideas and expressing their own clearly.

- CCSS.ELA-Literacy.SL.3.1a Come to discussions prepared, having read or studied required material; explicitly draw on that preparation and other information known about the topic to explore ideas under discussion.

- CCSS.ELA-Literacy.SL.3.1b Follow agreed-upon rules for discussions (e.g., gaining the floor in respectful ways, listening to others with care, speaking one at a time about the topics and texts under discussion).

- CCSS.ELA-Literacy.SL.3.1c Ask questions to check understanding of information presented, stay on topic, and link their comments to the remarks of others.

- CCSS.ELA-Literacy.SL.3.1d Explain their own ideas and understanding in light of the discussion.

Materials needed: Text book

Pencil

Paper

Time for lesson: 60 - 90 minutes

Lesson:

- Tell students they will be teachers for a day. Split students into groups of 2 to 5 (depending on chapter length).

- Explain to students that they must read the chapter and make notes on the most important information that needs shared.

- The students will then work together to share the information with the class. Explain to students that they can break the chapter up and each person present a section or all people can participate in all parts. If time permits and they are necessary, have students create visual aids.

Assessment: Assessment should be based on participation and presentation of appropriate information.

Lesson Two

Title: Sharing Skills

Topic: Presenting information to a group

Objective of lesson: Students will present information or teach a new skill to others.

Common Core State Standard used: SL 3.1 Engage effectively in a range of collaborative discussions (one-on-one, in groups, and teacher-led) with diverse partners on *grade 3 topics and texts*, building on others' ideas and expressing their own clearly.

- o CCSS.ELA-Literacy.SL.3.1a Come to discussions prepared having read or studied required material; explicitly draw on that preparation and other information known about the topic to explore ideas under discussion.

- o CCSS.ELA-Literacy.SL.3.1b Follow agreed-upon rules for discussions (e.g., gaining the floor in respectful ways, listening to others with care, speaking one at a time about the topics and texts under discussion).

- o CCSS.ELA-Literacy.SL.3.1c Ask questions to check understanding of information presented, stay on topic, and link their comments to the remarks of others.

- o CCSS.ELA-Literacy.SL.3.1d Explain their own ideas and understanding in light of the discussion.

Materials needed: None

Time for lesson: 30 - 60 minutes - each day

Lesson:

- Explain to students that they are all experts, but they are often experts in different things. Some people are knowledgeable about animals while others know how to shoot a basket from the three point line. Some may even be best at making silly faces or singing.

- No matter what the skill, students are going to share their knowledge with the whole class.

- Set aside a day when students can bring props or photos to teach others about their skill.

- Allow students to share the skill or knowledge and answer questions from the group.

Assessment: Assessment should be based on participation, including listening and sharing skills. (See speaking rubric)

Lesson One

Title: Chart Reading

Topic: Understanding diverse formats to gain knowledge

Objective of lesson: Students will use charts to answer questions.

Common Core State Standard used: SL 3.2 Determine the main ideas and supporting details of a text read aloud or information presented in diverse media and formats, including visually, quantitatively, and orally.

Materials needed: Charts (included)

Projector or sheet for each student

Time for lesson: 30 - 40 minutes

Lesson:

- Explain to students that often information is presented in a form other than writing, such as a chart or graph. Knowing how to answer questions using only charts and graphs can be important.

- Provide students with a copy of the charts or project on the board.

- Have students answer questions as a group or on paper. If answering as a group then have a student explain how they knew the answer.

Assessment: Assessment should be based on participation, including explanation.

Sample charts:

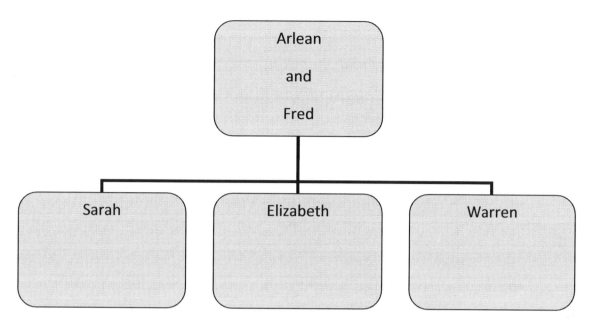

Parent/Child Chart

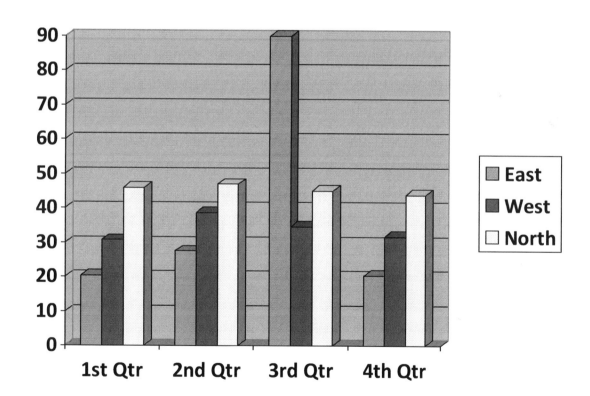

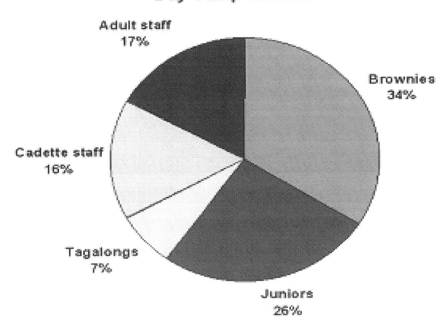

Questions:

1) Who were the parents of Elizabeth?

2) What percentage of Brownies attended day camp?

3) Which quarter was best for the East?

4) Which quarter was worst for the West?

5) Who are the siblings in the parent/child chart?

6) What percentage of Tagalongs were at day camp?

7) How many more brownies were at day camp than juniors?

8) Which area, North or East, stays most consistent throughout all four quarters?

Lesson Two

Title: Say What

Topic: Understanding diverse formats to gain knowledge

Objective of lesson: Students will determine the main idea of different media types.

Common Core State Standard used: SL 3.2 Determine the main ideas and supporting details of a text read aloud or information presented in diverse media and formats, including visually, quantitatively, and orally.

Materials needed: Access to the Internet with projector

Speakers

List of videos or other links (included)

Time for lesson: 30 - 45 minutes

Lesson:

- Tell students that you are going to spend a bit of time watching videos and commercials. Explain that sometimes the actual message is lost when using media formats.

- Show this video http://www.geico.com/about/commercials/ (Maxwell the pig)

- Stop the video just prior to the end and ask students what the commercial is advertising. Play the end. Ask students if they know what is being advertised now (Geiko insurance).

- Explain that, just like in the commercials, sometimes we have to read to the end of a paragraph to truly know what the main idea of the passage may be.

- Try a few more examples. Have students try to decide what is being advertised or talked about. Explain this is the main idea.

Assessment: Assessment should be based on participation.

Websites/Videos (find the main idea)

http://www.autoblog.com/2010/05/13/video-confusing-new-dodge-caravan-commercials-arent-helping/

http://www.youtube.com/watch?v=Mp4UtYNxZLg

http://www.youtube.com/watch?v=kfnXUWJzOsE

http://www.youtube.com/watch?v=NkuuZEey_bs

Lesson One

Title: Show and Tell Me More

Topic: Presenting and sharing information on a topic

Objective of lesson: Students will present and ask questions of other speakers.

Common Core State Standard used: SL 3.3 Ask and answer questions about information from a speaker, offering appropriate elaboration and detail.

Materials needed: Student will provide materials

Time for lesson: 20 - 30 (per week, per child)

Lesson:

- Students love to share their passion with others, so Show and Tell is a great way to practice speaking and asking questions.

- Assign 1 or 2 students weekly to be presenters. Explain that they can bring in any school appropriate prop or photos as needed to use for show and tell. (A letter home to the parents ahead of time is often useful)

- Allow students to explain their hobby, pastime, sport, etc. to the class and have at least three people ask questions to encourage the speaker further.

Assessment: Assessment should be based on participation of both the speaker and listeners.

Lesson Two

Title: See and Do

Topic: Learning a new skill based on visual media

Objective of lesson: Students will use visual media to learn a new skill.

Common Core State Standard used: SL 3.3 Ask and answer questions about information from a speaker, offering appropriate elaboration and detail.

Materials needed: Computer with Internet access

Paper

Scissors

Projection tool to show video

Time for lesson: 30 - 40 minutes

Lesson:

- Allow students to watch a simple video on an origami design. Pause after each section if needed. Have students watch and follow the video without assistance.

- Explain that some people are visual learners and a video can teach skills better than just reading.

Assessment: Assessment should be based on completing the design as shown in the video.

Video Links:

(frog) http://www.youtube.com/watch?v=uUkBjggLado

(butterfly) http://www.youtube.com/watch?v=SJOy7IduY8M

(elephant) http://on.aol.com/video/how-to-fold-an-origami-elephant-116056896

Lesson One

Title: Tell Me All About it

Topic: Sharing information

Objective of lesson: Students will orally report on a book they have or are reading.

Common Core State Standard used: SL 3.4 Report on a topic or text, tell a story, or recount an experience with appropriate facts and relevant, descriptive details, speaking clearly at an understandable pace.

Materials needed: Access to a library

Time for lesson: 15 -30 minutes and speaking part 5 -10 (per student)

Lesson:

- Allow students to visit the school library to choose a book on their given reading level.

- Have students spend time silently reading throughout the day or week with the goal of telling others about the book.

- Have students share a bit of what the book is about and whether or not they recommend reading the book for others.

Assessment: Assessment should be based on participation and clear presentation skills (see speaking rubric).

Lesson Two

Title: Book Club

Topic: Sharing ideas and insights

Objective of lesson: Students will work with a mini-book club, discussing the book and parts that they enjoyed or are confused by throughout.

Common Core State Standard used: SL 3.4 Report on a topic or text, tell a story, or recount an experience with appropriate facts and relevant, descriptive details, speaking clearly at an understandable pace.

Materials needed: Sets of reading level books

Time for lesson: 20-30 minutes (per week)

Lesson:

- Prior to beginning these activities explain the purpose of a book club. The purpose is to learn from each other what was interesting, what may be confusing, or what can be learned.

- Separate students into appropriate reading groups and provide a set of books (all the same book) for each child to read in that group.

- Students can read silently or in round robin style at your preference.

- Next have students discuss the book and what was liked, learned, misunderstood, or confusing. Also have the group decide whether they would recommend the book to others.

- Each week have a different member from each group share their discussion findings.

Assessment: Assessment should be based on participation and clear presentation skills (see speaking rubric).

Lesson One

Title: Can You Hear Me

Topic: Recording self to increase and improve fluid reading

Objective of lesson: Students will record themselves reading a familiar book or poem.

Common Core State Standard used: SL 3.5 Create engaging audio recordings of stories or poems that demonstrate fluid reading at an understandable pace; add visual displays when appropriate to emphasize or enhance certain facts or details.

Materials needed: Computers with audio recording or downloaded Audacity

Microphone

Headphones

Book or poem of choice

Time for lesson: 5 - 15 minutes per student

Lesson:

- Students are often surprised at how their voice actually sounds when reading. Have students choose a book or poem to record themselves reading.

- Allow children to listen to their own voice after finishing the recording and writing down what they could do to be a better reader.

- Allow rerecording if time permits.

Assessment: Assessment should be based on participation.

Free Audacity Download http://audacity.sourceforge.net/

Lesson Two

Title: Campfire Stories

Topic: Recording self to increase and improve fluid reading

Objective of lesson: Students will work with a group to create a scary story and record the story.

Common Core State Standard used: SL 3.5 Create engaging audio recordings of stories or poems that demonstrate fluid reading at an understandable pace; add visual displays when appropriate to emphasize or enhance certain facts or details.

Materials needed: Computers with audio recording or downloaded Audacity

Microphone

Headphones

Student created story

Time for lesson: 45-90 minutes

Lesson:

- Using a previously written story that is created by the students, allow students to record themselves reading in appropriate tones and voices. Also allow students to add sound effects as needed (scream for fear, laughter for funny, etc.).

- Set up a 'campfire' circle for students to listen to their recorded stories. (Offer popcorn or s'mores if allowed).

- After hearing the stories have students critique their work.

Assessment: Assessment should be based on participation.

Lesson One

Title: Can You Clarify

Topic: Adding detail for clarification

Objective of lesson: Students will add details to basic sentences.

Common Core State Standard used: SL 3.6 Speak in complete sentences when appropriate to task and situation in order to provide requested detail or clarification.

Materials needed: White board

Sample sentences (included)

Time for lesson: 30 - 45 minutes

Lesson:

- Project basic sentences onto the whiteboard. Explain to students that the sentences are very basic and would be better if more detailed.

- Offer this sample "The fox jumped over the log" to make the sentence more detailed and clear one could write "The red fox leapt quickly over the fallen dead log."

- Explain that more detail helps the reader gain a clearer understanding of a text. Offer students some basic sentences and allow each student to take a turn adding to the sentence until it is complete.

Assessment: Assessment should be based on creating more detailed sentences.

Simple Sentences

1) The cat lay down.

2) The girl sat in class.

3) The cow sat.

4) The dog ran.

5) The bird flapped.

6) The elephant stomped.

7) The horses took off.

8) The blanket was folded.

9) There was a pop.

10) The door opened.

Lesson Two

Title: Is It Complete

Topic: Identifying complete sentences

Objective of lesson: Students will identify partial and complete sentences.

Common Core State Standard used: SL 3.6 Speak in complete sentences when appropriate to task and situation in order to provide requested detail or clarification.

Materials needed: White board

Sample sentences (included)

Line paper if needed

Time for lesson: 20 - 30 minutes

Lesson:

- Using the white board, have students decide if sentences are complete or incomplete. For those that are incomplete have students make them complete sentences.

- Students could write new sentences on lined paper and turn in to teacher when finished.

Assessment: Assessment should be based on correctly identifying complete and incomplete sentences.

Sample Sentences

1) I walked up to the counter slowly.

2) Walked away quickly.

3) The breadsticks were.

4) The phone is ringing.

5) Sara stood up to.

6) We climbed the rugged mountain.

7) The ringing phone is.

8) The old house creaked when.

9) Please take out.

10) Please turn on the computer for me.

Lesson One

Title: Find Your Tense

Topic: Demonstrate knowledge of past, present, and future tense

Objective of lesson: Students will locate the past, present, and future tense of a sentence

Common Core State Standard used: L 3.1 Demonstrate command of the conventions of standard English grammar and usage when writing or speaking.

- CCSS.ELA-Literacy.L.3.1a Explain the function of nouns, pronouns, verbs, adjectives, and adverbs in general and their functions in particular sentences.

- CCSS.ELA-Literacy.L.3.1b Form and use regular and irregular plural nouns.

- CCSS.ELA-Literacy.L.3.1c Use abstract nouns (e.g., *childhood*).

- CCSS.ELA-Literacy.L.3.1d Form and use regular and irregular verbs.

- CCSS.ELA-Literacy.L.3.1e Form and use the simple (e.g., *I walked; I walk; I will walk*) verb tenses.

- CCSS.ELA-Literacy.L.3.1f Ensure subject-verb and pronoun-antecedent agreement.*

- CCSS.ELA-Literacy.L.3.1g Form and use comparative and superlative adjectives and adverbs, and choose between them depending on what is to be modified.

- CCSS.ELA-Literacy.L.3.1h Use coordinating and subordinating conjunctions.

- CCSS.ELA-Literacy.L.3.1i Produce simple, compound, and complex sentences.

Materials needed: Sentence cards (included)

Timer

Time for lesson: 5 minutes

Lesson:

- Offer students one of the included cards.

- Tell students that they must form a group with the people that have the past, present, and future of a given sentence.

- Set a timer for 30 seconds to see if students can find their partners.

Assessment: Assessment should be based on correctly and quickly finding partners.

Cut apart and hand out

He will go swimming.	He went swimming.	He is swimming.
The dog runs in circles.	The dog ran in circles.	The dog will run in circles.
We are going to the mall.	We went to the mall.	We are at the mall.
Which racer won?	Which racer will win?	Which racer is winning?
She will fold the clothes.	She is folding the clothes.	She folded the clothes.
The soda will go flat.	The soda is flat.	The soda went flat.
The cat will jump in the window.	The cat jumped in the window.	The cat jumps in the window.

Lesson Two

Title: Build a Sentence

Topic: Demonstrate knowledge of basic grammatical concepts

Objective of lesson: Students will build compound sentences from word blocks.

Common Core State Standard used: L 3.1 Demonstrate command of the conventions of standard English grammar and usage when writing or speaking.

- o CCSS.ELA-Literacy.L.3.1a Explain the function of nouns, pronouns, verbs, adjectives, and adverbs in general and their functions in particular sentences.

- o CCSS.ELA-Literacy.L.3.1b Form and use regular and irregular plural nouns.

- o CCSS.ELA-Literacy.L.3.1c Use abstract nouns (e.g., *childhood*).

- o CCSS.ELA-Literacy.L.3.1d Form and use regular and irregular verbs.

- o CCSS.ELA-Literacy.L.3.1e Form and use the simple (e.g., *I walked; I walk; I will walk*) verb tenses.

- o CCSS.ELA-Literacy.L.3.1f Ensure subject-verb and pronoun-antecedent agreement.*

- o CCSS.ELA-Literacy.L.3.1g Form and use comparative and superlative adjectives and adverbs, and choose between them depending on what is to be modified.

- o CCSS.ELA-Literacy.L.3.1h Use coordinating and subordinating conjunctions.

- o CCSS.ELA-Literacy.L.3.1i Produce simple, compound, and complex sentences.

Materials needed: Word tiles

Time for lesson: 15 minutes (per group)

Lesson:*Small groups are best

- Lay out word tiles on a large table. Have students in the group create at least three sentences each from the tiles.

- Continue the activity by asking students to make sentences around specific words or specific sentence types such as simple or compound.

Assessment: Assessment should be based on correctly building sentences.

Lesson One

Title: Minute to Win it

Topic: Demonstrate knowledge of basic grammatical concepts

Objective of lesson: Students will find errors in sentences within a time limit.

Common Core State Standard used: L 3.2 Demonstrate command of the conventions of standard English capitalization, punctuation, and spelling when writing.

- o CCSS.ELA-Literacy.L.3.2a Capitalize appropriate words in titles.

- o CCSS.ELA-Literacy.L.3.2b Use commas in addresses.

- o CCSS.ELA-Literacy.L.3.2c Use commas and quotation marks in dialogue.

- o CCSS.ELA-Literacy.L.3.2d Form and use possessives.

- o CCSS.ELA-Literacy.L.3.2e Use conventional spelling for high-frequency and other studied words and for adding suffixes to base words (e.g., *sitting, smiled, cries, happiness*).

- o CCSS.ELA-Literacy.L.3.2f Use spelling patterns and generalizations (e.g., *word families, position-based spellings, syllable patterns, ending rules, meaningful word parts*) in writing words.

- o CCSS.ELA-Literacy.L.3.2g Consult reference materials, including beginning dictionaries, as needed to check and correct spellings.

Materials needed: Board

Timer

Time for lesson: 1 minute (per day)

Lesson:*Great warm-up activity

- Each morning have at least three sentences on the board that are covered or on a paper that is face down on each desk. Three to four errors should be in each sentence.

- Set a timer for one minute and have students look at the paper and circle each correction that needs to be made. If using the board have students write the corrections on their paper, but set the timer to 2 minutes.

Assessment: Assessment should be based on number of corrections made or found and improvement over time.

Lesson Two

Title: Passing Notes

Topic: Demonstrate knowledge of basic grammatical concepts

Objective of lesson: Students will write out a brief conversation using appropriate markings.

Common Core State Standard used: L 3.2 Demonstrate command of the conventions of standard English capitalization, punctuation, and spelling when writing.

- o <u>CCSS.ELA-Literacy.L.3.2a</u> Capitalize appropriate words in titles.

- o <u>CCSS.ELA-Literacy.L.3.2b</u> Use commas in addresses.

- o <u>CCSS.ELA-Literacy.L.3.2c</u> Use commas and quotation marks in dialogue.

- o <u>CCSS.ELA-Literacy.L.3.2d</u> Form and use possessives.

- o <u>CCSS.ELA-Literacy.L.3.2e</u> Use conventional spelling for high-frequency and other studied words and for adding suffixes to base words (e.g., *sitting, smiled, cries, happiness*).

- o <u>CCSS.ELA-Literacy.L.3.2f</u> Use spelling patterns and generalizations (e.g., *word families, position-based spellings, syllable patterns, ending rules, meaningful word parts*) in writing words.

- o <u>CCSS.ELA-Literacy.L.3.2g</u> Consult reference materials, including beginning dictionaries, as needed to check and correct spellings.

Materials needed: Paper

Pencil

Time for lesson: 15 - 30 minutes

Lesson:*Great warm-up activity

- Write the following on the board "How are you today?" asked the teacher.

- Ask a few students how they would answer. Write the responses correctly on the board. Point out quotation marks, commas, and punctuation.

- Now write a second question on the board. "What did you do last night?" asked _____ (have students fill in their name). Have students pass the paper to a partner to answer, also using dialogue in text. Allow students to continue the written conversation until each has written at least three dialogue sentences.

Assessment: Assessment should be based on participation.

Lesson One

Title: Crossword Madness

Topic: Synonyms and antonyms

Objective of lesson: Students will use synonyms and antonyms to fill in a crossword puzzle.

Common Core State Standard used: L 3.3 Use knowledge of language and its conventions when writing, speaking, reading, or listening.

- CCSS.ELA-Literacy.L.3.3a Choose words and phrases for effect.*

- CCSS.ELA-Literacy.L.3.3b Recognize and observe differences between the conventions of spoken and written standard English.

Materials needed: Crossword puzzle (sample included)

Time for lesson: 30 - 40 minutes

Lesson:

- Make sure students understand the concept of antonyms and synonyms before handing over the puzzle.

- Students will be expected to think of synonyms and antonyms for each clue to see if they properly fit in the right blank.

- A word bank can be included in case students struggle.

Assessment: Assessment should be based on finding appropriate words for the blanks.

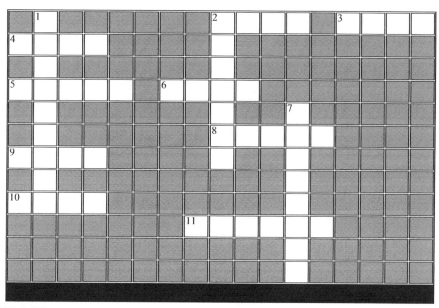

ACROSS

2. antonym for soft
3. antonym for short
4. synonym for nice
5. antonym for dark
6. antonym for bright
8. antonym for bald
9. synonym for big
10. antonym for nice
11. antonym for solid

DOWN

1. synonym for small
2. antonym for sick
7. synonym for very cold

huge	tall	hard	mean
miniature	dull	hairy	kind
healthy	freezing	liquid	light

*Puzzles for your class can be created and printed for free at
http://www.crosswordpuzzlegames.com/create.html

Lesson Two

Title: Draw Me the Difference

Topic: Understanding word choices have meaning and effect

Objective of lesson: Students will illustrate the differences between synonyms.

Common Core State Standard used: L 3.3 Use knowledge of language and its conventions when writing, speaking, reading, or listening.

   o   CCSS.ELA-Literacy.L.3.3a Choose words and phrases for effect.*

   o   CCSS.ELA-Literacy.L.3.3b Recognize and observe differences between the conventions of spoken and written standard English.

Materials needed: Drawing paper

Art supplies

Comparable synonyms (included)

Time for lesson: 30 - 45 minutes

Lesson: (Best for small groups)

- Explain to students that synonyms are words that mean about the same thing, but that using one word over another can give the reader a different picture of what is being said.

- Hand students some paper and a marker of crayons. Ask students to draw a small bug on the paper. When they are finished, ask them to draw a tiny bug. (The tiny bug should be smaller). Explain that these are synonyms but one word brings up a different picture than the other.

- Now try a few more synonyms as pictures. Have students fold a second sheet of paper (or use the back of the first one) into eight squares. Each square will hold a picture to represent the given word.

Assessment: Assessment should be based on appropriate drawings to indicate understanding.

Synonym pairs (use as many or as few as you want and add a noun to each (i.e. a big monster, huge monster))

big, huge

mad, furious

happy, ecstatic

crying, sobbing

young, baby

sad, depressed

tall, enormous

funny, hilarious

Lesson One

Title: If, Then

Topic: Adding affixes to words

Objective of lesson: Students will add common affixes to words and determine meaning of the new word (real and nonsense)

Common Core State Standard used: L 3.4 Determine or clarify the meaning of unknown and multiple-meaning word and phrases based on grade 3 reading and content, choosing flexibly from a range of strategies.

- o CCSS.ELA-Literacy.L.3.4a Use sentence-level context as a clue to the meaning of a word or phrase.

- o CCSS.ELA-Literacy.L.3.4b Determine the meaning of the new word formed when a known affix is added to a known word (e.g., *agreeable/disagreeable, comfortable/uncomfortable, care/careless, heat/preheat*).

- o CCSS.ELA-Literacy.L.3.4c Use a known root word as a clue to the meaning of an unknown word with the same root (e.g., *company, companion*).

- o CCSS.ELA-Literacy.L.3.4d Use glossaries or beginning dictionaries, both print and digital, to determine or clarify the precise meaning of key words and phrases.

Materials needed: Pencil

Worksheet (included)

Affix list (included)

Time for lesson: 30 - 45 minutes

Lesson:

- Project or list affixes and meanings on the board. Explain to students that affixes are attached to base words to form new words. These new words usually carry new meanings, but the base word is always a hint to the meaning.

- Offer the following example: What does comfort mean? What does comfortable mean? What does uncomfortable mean? –able and un are both affixes that change the meaning of the word, but the base word hints at the overall meaning.

- Let's review some common affixes before trying some individually. Review list.

- Hand out worksheet and explain to students that the base word and affixes are given and they need to write the new word and what it means.

Assessment: Assessment should be based on correct answers.

Common Affixes:

Affix	Meaning		
mis-	wrongly	pre-	before
pro-	favor, forward	re-	again, back
un-	not	-ed	past-tense
-er	more	-est	most
-ing	present participle	-ly	like, resembling
-y	being or having		

Write the new word and the meaning

Sample: mis +take = mistake meaning to take wrongly

1. fun + y = _____ meaning _____

2. pro + active = _____ meaning _____

3. big + er = _____ meaning _____

4. un + tie = _____ meaning _____

5. friend + ly = _____ meaning _____

Write the affix and base word for each new word

6. _____ + _____ = largest

7. _____ + _____ = fruity

8. _____ + _____ = misbehave

9. _____ + _____ = playing

10. _____ + _____ = pretest

Write the word that would mean the following

11. to use wrongly _____

12. to do every month _____

13. to paint again _____

14. before becoming a teen _____

Lesson Two

Title: Race to the Meaning

Topic: Using base words to determine definitions

Objective of lesson: Students will use base words to determine meaning

Common Core State Standard used: L 3.4 Determine or clarify the meaning of unknown and multiple-meaning word and phrases based on grade 3 reading and content, choosing flexibly from a range of strategies.

- CCSS.ELA-Literacy.L.3.4a Use sentence-level context as a clue to the meaning of a word or phrase.

- CCSS.ELA-Literacy.L.3.4b Determine the meaning of the new word formed when a known affix is added to a known word (e.g., *agreeable/disagreeable, comfortable/uncomfortable, care/careless, heat/preheat*).

- CCSS.ELA-Literacy.L.3.4c Use a known root word as a clue to the meaning of an unknown word with the same root (e.g., *company, companion*).

- CCSS.ELA-Literacy.L.3.4d Use glossaries or beginning dictionaries, both print and digital, to determine or clarify the precise meaning of key words and phrases.

Materials needed: Index cards with definitions

Index cards with unfamiliar words

Time for lesson: 15 - 30 minutes –can do several times

Lesson:

- Clip definitions that have been written on index cards to a wall or place on empty desks. Have matching index cards for students that have words that match the definitions.

- Explain to students that when you say go, they will have 1 minutes to find the definition that matches their word card. Explain that the word on the card may be unfamiliar, but using the base word can help determine meaning. *This is great for vocabulary words, spelling words, and affix practice.

- If the area is limited, split students into teams and have one person go at a time from each team or use small groups. This can also be done in a gym for added activity.

Assessment: Assessment should be based on participation and correct matching.

Lesson One

Title: Word Play

Topic: Using literal meanings to determine phrases in a word game.

Objective of lesson: Students will decode word games to determine meanings.

Common Core State Standard used: L 3.5 Demonstrate understanding of figurative language, word relationships and nuances in word meanings.

- CCSS.ELA-Literacy.L.3.5a Distinguish the literal and nonliteral meanings of words and phrases in context (e.g., *take steps*).

- CCSS.ELA-Literacy.L.3.5b Identify real-life connections between words and their use (e.g., describe people who are *friendly* or *helpful*).

- CCSS.ELA-Literacy.L.3.5c Distinguish shades of meaning among related words that describe states of mind or degrees of certainty (e.g., *knew, believed, suspected, heard, wondered*).

Materials needed: Word play worksheet

Time for lesson: 30 - 40 minutes

Lesson:

- Explain to students that much of what we say is not literal. We do not literally mean it is raining cats and dogs, but that is a common phrase.

- Tell students they are going to have to think literally for the next activity. They will use pictures to find common phrases. Use the following examples "themidIMdle" means I'm stuck in the middle or <u>stand</u>

    I means I understand.

- Allow students to try some on their own.

Assessment: Assessment should be based on participation.

Find examples to print here http://myfunteacher.com/plexers/plexers1_60.pdf

Answers: http://myfunteacher.com/plexers/plexerAnswers1_60.pdf

Lesson Two

Title: Shades of Grey

Topic: Distinguishing shades of meaning for similar words

Objective of lesson: Students will determine shades of meaning on a scale.

Common Core State Standard used: L 3.5 Demonstrate understanding of figurative language, word relationships and nuances in word meanings.

- CCSS.ELA-Literacy.L.3.5a Distinguish the literal and nonliteral meanings of words and phrases in context (e.g., *take steps*).

- CCSS.ELA-Literacy.L.3.5b Identify real-life connections between words and their use (e.g., describe people who are *friendly* or *helpful*).

- CCSS.ELA-Literacy.L.3.5c Distinguish shades of meaning among related words that describe states of mind or degrees of certainty (e.g., *knew, believed, suspected, heard, wondered*).

Materials needed: Word list (included)

Scale (included)

Time for lesson: 20 - 30 minutes

Lesson:

- Explain to students that sometimes we use words for effect. Saying something is big is different from something being enormous. Though these words mean almost the same thing there are shades of different meanings.

- Offer students a copy of the included grey scale and explain that they are going to rank words. Words that are stronger will go on the darker end. Off this example (Ranked in order from light to dark: big, large, huge, enormous)

- Give students other lists of words to rank.

Assessment: Assessment should be based on participation.

Grey Scale:

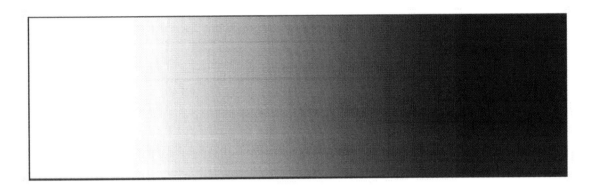

Sample Words: (Unranked)

1. small, tiny, little, miniature, petite

2. large, bulky, hefty, fat, obese

3. pretty, attractive, beautiful, cute

4. mad, angry, furious, livid

5. sad, gloomy, miserable, depressed

6. happy, content, joyful, cheery, ecstatic

7. tall, elevated, giant, soaring, lofty

Mathematics

Lesson One

Title: If This, Than That

Topic: Interpret products as whole numbers

Objective of lesson: Students will learn to group objects to demonstrate multiplication facts.

Common Core State Standard used: OAA 3.1 Interpret products of whole numbers, e.g., interpret 5 × 7 as the total number of objects in 5 groups of 7 objects each. *For example, describe a context in which a total number of objects can be expressed as 5 × 7.*

Materials needed:

Time for lesson: 30 - 45 minutes

Lesson:

- Split students into pairs for this activity

- Offer students 100 of any given object (blocks, paper clips, cotton, sticks, etc)

- Explain that multiplication is much like addition in that you can count groups of objects so 5 times 7 is the same as 7 groups of 5 or 5 groups of 7 and can be shown with objects.

- Offer students multiplication problems and have them represent them with the objects. Each partner should show it in a different manner.

- You can have partners practice with many different problems.

Assessment: Assessment should be based on participation and correct grouping.

Lesson Two

Title: Teach Me to Separate

Topic: Interpret products as whole numbers

Objective of lesson: Students will learn to group objects to demonstrate multiplication facts.

Common Core State Standard used: OAA 3.1 Interpret products of whole numbers, e.g., interpret 5 × 7 as the total number of objects in 5 groups of 7 objects each. *For example, describe a context in which a total number of objects can be expressed as 5 × 7.*

Materials needed: Board

Paper

Pencil

Sorting objects

Time for lesson: 5 -10 minutes per student

Lesson:

- Have students split into groups of three or four.

- Explain that they will be the teachers today and create multiplication problems that can be solved by grouping. However, they must also show how to solve each problem and group it in two different ways for the class.

- Allow groups to write 3 to 5 problems and then show the class how to work out each problem on the board or overhead.

Assessment: Assessment should be based on participation and correct grouping.

Lesson One

Title: Total Cut Up

Topic: Equal partitioning

Objective of lesson: Students will cut objects to correctly represent equal shares of an object.

Common Core State Standard used: OAA 3.2 Interpret whole-number quotients of whole numbers, e.g., interpret 56 ÷ 8 as the number of objects in each share when 56 objects are partitioned equally into 8 shares, or as a number of shares when 56 objects are partitioned into equal shares of 8 objects each. *For example, describe a context in which a number of shares or a number of groups can be expressed as 56 ÷ 8.*

Materials needed: Paper

Scissors

Time for lesson: 20 - 30 minutes

Lesson: (Best in small groups)

- This exercise is best practiced in small groups; so that it can continuity be monitored.

- Explain to students that in division, shares of a number are represented. So a problem such as 6/2 is actually 6 objects divided into 2 equal groups.

- So have students cut 6 equally sized squares and sort into 2 equal groups. How many does each group have? 3 that is simple division.

- Continue with several problems. Save squares for later practice.

Assessment: Assessment should be based on participation and correct partitioning.

Lesson Two

Title: Color Me Divided

Topic: Equal partitioning

Objective of lesson: Students will color blocks to show equal partitioning

Common Core State Standard used: OAA 3.2 Interpret whole-number quotients of whole numbers, e.g., interpret 56 ÷ 8 as the number of objects in each share when 56 objects are partitioned equally into 8 shares, or as a number of shares when 56 objects are partitioned into equal shares of 8 objects each. *For example, describe a context in which a number of shares or a number of groups can be expressed as 56 ÷ 8.*

Materials needed: Graph paper

Crayons/colored pencils

Time for lesson: 20 - 30 minutes

Lesson: (Best in small groups)

- This exercise is best practiced in small groups, so it can be continuity monitored.

- Explain to students that in division, shares of a number are represented. So a problem such as 6/2 is actually 6 objects divided into 2 equal groups.

- Have students use graph paper to represent division problems (sample included)

- Have students attempt several problems to monitor understanding.

- Students can continue to use in small groups to reinforce skill.

Assessment: Assessment should be based on participation and correct partitioning.

8/4 = 8 divided equally into 4 parts so groups of 2 (use different colors for each group)

Lesson One

Title: Work it Out

Topic: Solving word problems with illustrations

Objective of lesson: Students will work word problems utilizing multiplication and division.

Common Core State Standard used: OAA 3.3 Use multiplication and division within 100 to solve word problems in situations involving equal groups, arrays, and measurement quantities, e.g., by using drawings and equations with a symbol for the unknown number to represent the problem.

Materials needed: Pencil

Worksheet (included)

Time for lesson: 30 - 40 minutes

Lesson:

- Explain to students that word problems can best be solved by taking them one step at a time and drawing pictures to help with the math function. This includes division and multiplication.

- Offer students an example before giving out the included worksheet that has both multiplication and division word problems.

Assessment: Assessment should be based on correct answers.

Answers:

1) 10

2) 68

3) 7

4) 21

Sample Word Problems:

1) Amanda had 100 apples that she had picked over the weekend at the orchard. Since she could not eat all those apples, she decided to share with friends. If she kept 10 apples for herself and then equally shared with 9 friends, how many apples did each friend receive? _____

2) Sara decided to make gifts for her party. She had 2 made for each guest. She had 34 guests coming in all. How many gifts did Sara make?

_____

3) Jeffery got a mark on his behavior chart each time he yelled out in class. Jeffery received 35 marks in a normal school week. He received the same number of marks each day. How many marks did he receive each day? _____

4) The class was drawing pictures for a sick youngster. Each student drew 3 pictures to brighter her day. The class created a total of 63 pictures. How many people are in the class? _____

Lesson One

Title: Show Me a Problem

Topic: Multiplication and division word problems

Objective of lesson: Students will create word problems using fellow students.

Common Core State Standard used: OAA 3.3 Use multiplication and division within 100 to solve word problems in situations involving equal groups, arrays, and measurement quantities, e.g., by using drawings and equations with a symbol for the unknown number to represent the problem.

Materials needed: Pencil

Paper (or math journal)

Time for lesson: 10-30 minutes

Lesson:

- Allow students to work alone or in pairs to create a word problem that uses division or multiplication.

- Have students demonstrate the word problem using objects in the room and other students to show the solution.

Assessment: Assessment should be based on creating a valid word problem that can be demonstrated.

Lesson One

Title: What's Missing

Topic: Determining unknown numbers in multiplication and division.

Objective of lesson: Students will identify missing numbers correctly in given problems.

Common Core State Standard used: OAA 3.4 Determine the unknown whole number in a multiplication or division equation relating three whole numbers. *For example, determine the unknown number that makes the equation true in each of the equations 8 × ? = 48, 5 = _ ÷ 3, 6 × 6 = ?*

Materials needed: 2 decks of cards (face cards and joker removed)

Division and multiplication problems (digit missing)

Time for lesson: 10-15 minutes (per group)

Lesson: (Small groups)

- Deal 10-12 cards to each student. Explain that the cards are just like numbers in math except aces act as ones.

- Offer multiplication and division problems with a missing number.

- Have children raise their hand if one of their cards solves the problem. If no one has a card to solve the problem have everyone draw until an answer is found.

Assessment: Assessment should be based on correct answers and participation.

Lesson Two

Title: Multiplication Madness

Topic: Determining unknown numbers in multiplication problems.

Objective of lesson: Students will identify missing numbers correctly in given problems.

Common Core State Standard used: OAA 3.4 Determine the unknown whole number in a multiplication or division equation relating three whole numbers. *For example, determine the unknown number that makes the equation true in each of the equations 8 × ? = 48, 5 = _ ÷ 3, 6 × 6 = ?*

Materials needed: Index cards (3 sets with the digits 1-10 per each set)

Sentence strips with multiplication problems with a missing digit

Time for lesson: 5 minutes (per group) and 15 – 30 whole group

Lesson:

- Place sentence strips with problems around the room. Randomly hand out numbers written on index cards. Have students leave their backs turned until you say go.

- Set a timer, when you say go, have students find a problem in which their number will correctly solve the problem. *Use small groups or have one problem per number handed out.

- Review all problems with the class.

Assessment: Assessment should be based on correct answers and participation.

Lesson One

Title: We Are Breaking Up

Topic: Distributive property

Objective of lesson: Students will use the distributive property to break apart numbers based on multiplication properties.

Common Core State Standard used: OAA 3.5 Apply properties of operations as strategies to multiply and divide.[2] *Examples: If 6 × 4 = 24 is known, then 4 × 6 = 24 is also known. (Commutative property of multiplication.) 3 × 5 × 2 can be found by 3 × 5 = 15, then 15 × 2 = 30, or by 5 × 2 = 10, then 3 × 10 = 30. (Associative property of multiplication.) Knowing that 8 × 5 = 40 and 8 × 2 = 16, one can find 8 × 7 as 8 × (5 + 2) = (8 × 5) + (8 × 2) = 40 + 16 = 56. (Distributive property.)*

Materials needed: White board

Index cards (or number blocks)

Time for lesson: 5-20 minutes

Lesson:

- Before beginning this lesson in which students will come up one at a time, offer an example. (See below)

- On a white board (or transparency) offer students a number to break down into at least two different forms of a multiplication problem. Though this is not the actual distributive property it is the beginning to understanding.

- Allow each student to try at least one.

Assessment: Assessment should be based on correct breakdown of large numbers.

Sample

40 = (8 x 5) or (4 x 10) or (2 x 20)

Lesson Two

Title: Joined At the Hip

Topic: Commutative property

Objective of lesson: Students will use the commutative property to group numbers and make multiplication simpler.

Common Core State Standard used: OAA 3.5 Apply properties of operations as strategies to multiply and divide.[2] *Examples: If 6 × 4 = 24 is known, then 4 × 6 = 24 is also known. (Commutative property of multiplication.) 3 × 5 × 2 can be found by 3 × 5 = 15, then 15 × 2 = 30, or by 5 × 2 = 10, then 3 × 10 = 30. (Associative property of multiplication.) Knowing that 8 × 5 = 40 and 8 × 2 = 16, one can find 8 × 7 as 8 × (5 + 2) = (8 × 5) + (8 × 2) = 40 + 16 = 56. (Distributive property.)*

Materials needed: Mini dry erase boards

Dry erase markers

Erasers (or paper towels)

Time for lesson: 30 - 45 minutes

Lesson:

- Before beginning this lesson in which students will come up one at a time, offer an example. (See below)

- On their mini white boards have students write a sample problem and use the commutative property to solve. Remind students that as long as all the numbers are used it does not matter how they are grouped to solve the problem.

- Once the problem is solved, have students hold up their boards to check answers.

- Have students pair share with partners or work in small groups.

- Monitors groups and help where needed.

Assessment: Assessment should be based on correct breakdown of problems and correct answers.

Lesson One

Title: Turn it Around

Topic: Using multiplication to solve division problems

Objective of lesson: Students will use multiplication facts to solve division problems.

Common Core State Standard used: OAA 3.6 Understand division as an unknown-factor problem. *For example, find 32 ÷ 8 by finding the number that makes 32 when multiplied by 8.*

Materials needed: Multiplication chart

Division problems

Dry erase boards for each student

Dry erase markers

Paper towels (erasers)

Time for lesson: 30 - 40 minutes

Lesson:

- Explain to students that sometimes it is easier to turn division problems into missing number multiplication problems to solve. Give the following example. 32/8 = or 32=8 x _____ If the missing number is found then the problem is solved. So 8 times 4 equals 32 and 32/8 equals 4.

- Allow students to try problems on their own. After each problem is worked, have students display work on the small dry erase boards for assessment.

- Assessment: Assessment should be based on correct breakdown of problems and correct answers.

Lesson Two

Title: Change It Up

Topic: Using multiplication to solve division problems

Objective of lesson: Students will use multiplication facts to solve division problems.

Common Core State Standard used: OAA 3.6 Understand division as an unknown-factor problem. *For example, find 32 ÷ 8 by finding the number that makes 32 when multiplied by 8.*

Materials needed: Paper or large cards (printed with numbers and multiplication/division signs)

Division problems

Time for lesson: 20 - 30 minutes

Lesson:

- Explain to students that sometimes it is easier to turn division problems into missing number multiplication problems to solve. Give the following example. 32/8 = or 32=8 x _____ If the missing number is found then the problem is solved. So 8 times 4 is 32 and 32/8 is 4.

- Choose several students to represent a division problem. Have each student hold up a card with the number on it and a division sign in the middle.

- Now have a student use other students and cards to turn the problem into a missing number multiplication problem and solve by placing more students.

- As students become proficient, allow them to make up problems. This allows students to get up and move while practicing math skills.

Assessment: Assessment should be based on correct breakdown of problems, participation, and correct answers.

Lesson One

Title: Multiplication Baseball

Topic: Practicing multiplication

Objective of lesson: Students will answer multiplication questions without hesitation.

Common Core State Standard used: OAA 3.7 Fluently multiply and divide within 100, using strategies such as the relationship between multiplication and division (e.g., knowing that 8 × 5 = 40, one knows 40 ÷ 5 = 8) or properties of operations. By the end of Grade 3, know from memory all products of two one-digit numbers.

Materials needed: 4 desks

Time for lesson: 20 - 30 minutes

Lesson:

- Set four desks up or other objects in a baseball diamond pattern

- Split class into two teams and explain the following: Multiplication baseball requires you to answer multiplication questions quickly. The teacher will 'pitch' (say) a multiplication problem and the 'batter' must answer immediately. Hesitation means an out, but a correct answer means take a base. There is only 1 out allowed per round and then the other team gets a chance. The game will continue until time is called or nine innings.

- Begin playing multiplication baseball.

Assessment: Assessment should be based on correct answers and participation.

Lesson Two

Title: Division Basketball

Topic: Practicing division within 100

Objective of lesson: Students will answer division problems and then try to score points for their 'team'

Common Core State Standard used: OAA 3.7 Fluently multiply and divide within 100, using strategies such as the relationship between multiplication and division (e.g., knowing that 8 × 5 = 40, one knows 40 ÷ 5 = 8) or properties of operations. By the end of Grade 3, know from memory all products of two one-digit numbers.

Materials needed: Masking tape

3 trash cans or other containers (labeled 1, 2, and 3)

Paper or small balls

Time for lesson: 20 - 30 minutes

Lesson:

- Split students into two teams and explain the following rules: Division basketball is not just about division, it is about decision making. A member of each team will work the same division problem. Those who get the answer correct will get the opportunity to take a 'shot' for their team. If the answer is wrong, no shot is offered. If correct the member must choose whether to shoot for the 1, 2, or 3 point basket. If that basket is made, that number of points is awarded; if not then no points are awarded. Making the wrong basket does not give any points.

- Allow students to play division basketball.

Assessment: Assessment should be based on correct answers and participation.

Baskets should be placed different distances from a marked point on the floor, with 3 points being the furthest away.

X – tape mark

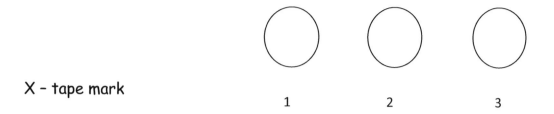

1   2   3

Lesson One

Title: Step by Step

Topic: Solving two step word problems

Objective of lesson: Students will answer two step word problems.

Common Core State Standard used: OAA 3.8 Solve two-step word problems using the four operations. Represent these problems using equations with a letter standing for the unknown quantity. Assess the reasonableness of answers using mental computation and estimation strategies including rounding.

Materials needed: Step organizer (sample included)

Word problems (samples included)

Time for lesson: 30 - 40 minutes

Lesson:

- Explain to students that sometimes word problems get confusing, but if you take it step by step then the right answer can be determined. Give the following example: Myles had 35 pencils he wanted to share with friends. He wanted each of his five friends to have an equal share. So he handed them out, but then two more friends showed up. Myles has to rearrange so everyone can have an equal number of pencils. How many pencils will each person get?

- Explain that the problem must be taken step by step; just like walking down a flight of stairs it should be taken one piece at a time. break apart a problem for students (sample below)

- Allow students to work several other problems using the step organizer if desired.

Assessment: Assessment should be based on correct answers.

Sample Problem:

35 pencils with 5 friends

2 more friends

add to make 7 friends

divide total 35 pencils by 7 friends

each friend gets 5 pencils

Sample Two Step Problems

1) Andy is learning to type. He can type 20 words a minute. How long will it take him to type is 80 word story?

2) It is 7:45 AM and you are having a party at 2:30 PM. How many hours and minutes do you have to wait before the party?

3) You have $42.50 saved for a new skateboard that costs $56.50. How much more money is needed before you can buy the skateboard?

4) There are 20 legs in my back yard, but I am only counting dogs. Now I see 30 legs, but the children from next door have come over to visit. How many dogs and children are in my yard?

5) If you ate a pizza and a half in a day and a half. How many pizzas would you eat in 7 days?

6) You have paid the cashier 2 twenty dollar bills on a bill that was $32.50. How much change will you receive?

7) A caterpillar is trying to crawl up a tree. It takes 2 minutes to climb 1 foot, but it falls back 6 inches each time it reaches 1 foot. How long will it take the caterpillar to crawl to the top of the 6 foot tree?

Lesson Two

Title: What is Needed

Topic: Solving two step word problems, by identifying the unknown

Objective of lesson: Students will answer two step word problems.

Common Core State Standard used: OAA 3.8 Solve two-step word problems using the four operations. Represent these problems using equations with a letter standing for the unknown quantity. Assess the reasonableness of answers using mental computation and estimation strategies including rounding.

Materials needed: Word problems (at least two step)

Pencils

Highlighters

Time for lesson: 20 - 30 minutes

Lesson:

- Explain to students that sometimes word problems are hard to understand, but they can be figured out if you take things slowly.

- This activity is just about finding out what is needed because often, word problems are confusing or offer unnecessary information.

- Help students work through several problems by highlighting important information and marking out what is not important such as names, animals, etc. *This can help students who are ADHD or have processing disorders to search for just important information.

Assessment: Assessment should be based on participation and understanding.

Lesson One

Title: Mathematical Magic

Topic: Identifying patterns in math

Objective of lesson: Students will learn about identifiable patterns in math.

Common Core State Standard used: OAA 3.9 Identify arithmetic patterns (including patterns in the addition table or multiplication table), and explain them using properties of operations. *For example, observe that 4 times a number is always even, and explain why 4 times a number can be decomposed into two equal addends.*

Materials needed: Math journals (optional)

Time for lesson: 5 minutes (sharing a new trick each day)

Lesson:

- Each morning or during math time, share a new trick with students. If math journals are kept, have students record the trick and test it. Explain that there are many ways to find answers to a problem. Have students work with a partner to see if they have two different ways to answer a question.

- Assessment: Assessment should be based on participation only.

Math Tips and Tricks:

1) To multiply by 9, try this:
(1) Spread your two hands out and place them on a desk or table in front of you.
(2) To multiply by 3, fold down the 3rd finger from the left. To multiply by 4, it would be the 4th finger and so on.
(3) the answer is 27 ... READ it from the two fingers on the left of the folded

down finger and the 7 fingers on the right of it.

This works for anything up to 9x10!

2) To multiply any two digit number by 11:

- For this example we will use 54.

- Separate the two digits in you mind (5__4).

- Notice the hole between them!

- Add the 5 and the 4 together (5+4=9)

- Put the resulting 9 in the hole 594. That's it! 11 x 54=594

The only thing tricky to remember is that if the result of the addition is greater than 9, you only put the "ones" digit in the hole and carry the "tens" digit from the addition. For example 11 x 57 ... 5__7 ... 5+7=12 ... put the 2 in the hole and add the 1 from the 12 to the 5 in to get 6 for a result of 627 ... 11 x 57 = 627

3) (6,7,8,9,10 multiplication) Place your fingers as in the below image and consider the value of fingers in each hand to be 6, 7, 8, 9 and 10 - in the order from small finger to thumb.

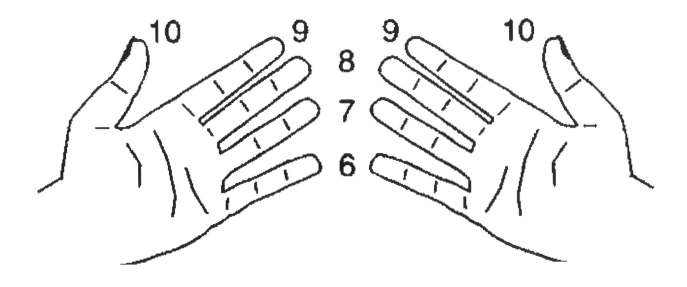

Example

Consider the multiplication of **7 × 8**.

Make the finger numbered 7 in the left hand to touch the finger numbered 8 in the right hand.

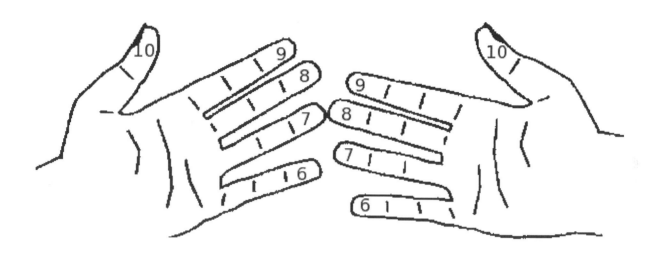

Step 1:

Now in the left hand, count the finger which is touching (7) and the ones below that = 2 fingers

Similarly in the right hand, count the finger which is touching (8) and the ones below that = 3 fingers

Add the above counted fingers = 2 + 3 = 5 fingers

Multiply the number by 10 = 5 × 10 = 50 -----> (1)

Step 2:

In the left hand, count the fingers above the touching finger = 3 fingers

Similarly in the right hand, count the fingers above the touching finger = 2 fingers

Multiply both = 3 × 2 = 6 -----> (2)

Step 3:

Add (1) and (2),

= 50 + 6 = 56

So, the answer for **7 × 8 = 56** which is easily found through the above trick.

Lesson Two

Title: Pattern Hunt

Topic: Identifying patterns in math

Objective of lesson: Students will learn about identifiable patterns in math.

Common Core State Standard used: OAA 3.9 Identify arithmetic patterns (including patterns in the addition table or multiplication table), and explain them using properties of operations. *For example, observe that 4 times a number is always even, and explain why 4 times a number can be decomposed into two equal addends.*

Materials needed: Multiplication chart

Crayons (pencils, markers)

Time for lesson: 25 – 30 minutes

Lesson: (Place in pairs)

- Explain to students that the multiplication table is filled with patterns.

- Allow students to work in pairs with a highlighter or crayon and try to find and color in patterns. Make sure a different color is used for each new pattern.

- Allow groups to compare patterns with the class.

Assessment: Assessment should be based on participation only.

Lesson One

Title: Round It Up

Topic: Rounding to the nearest 10 or 100's spot

Objective of lesson: Students will round to the nearest tens and hundreds.

Common Core State Standard used: NBT 3.1 Use place value understanding to round whole numbers to the nearest 10 or 100.

Materials needed: Number flip charts (instructions included)

Index card books (spiral bound) Make ahead

Markers

Time for lesson: 30 - 40

Lesson:

- Using the individualized number flip charts, call out a three digit number and have students round the number to the nearest ten or hundred at your discretion.

- Repeat for several numbers. Have students hold up answers.

Assessment: Assessment should be based on correct rounding.

Number Flip Book

1) Using an index card book (spiral bound) cut each card into three sections, leaving the spirals intact. If spiral index books are not available, cut regular index cards, punch holes at the tops and tie them together with ribbon.

2) On each card write the digits 0-9, one number on each card.

3) Use as a flip book.

spirals---------------------------

| 1 | c u t h e r e | 2 | c u t h e r e | 3 |

Lesson Two

Title: Stand Up, Sit Down, Round

Topic: Rounding up or down to the nearest tens or hundreds spot.

Objective of lesson: Students will round in the tens and hundreds place.

Common Core State Standard used: NBT 3.1 Use place value understanding to round whole numbers to the nearest 10 or 100.

Materials needed: Room for students to move around

Time for lesson: 30 - 40 minutes

Lesson:

- Remind students that numbers under 5 are rounded down and numbers 5 and over are rounded up.

- Tell students you will give them a number like 15 and ask what the number would be rounded to (20). Explain that if the number is rounded up then you want them to stand, but if it should be rounded down then they should sit (or remain in position if it is the same as the previous one).

- Try another example where students stand or sit and then start the game.

- Have a student become teacher, continue for practice.

- Continue trying numbers until students become disinterested.

Assessment: Assessment should be based on correct rounding up or down.

Lesson One

Title: Race to the Right Answer

Topic: Adding and subtracting within 1000

Objective of lesson: Students will work as a team to add and subtract numbers within 1000

Common Core State Standard used: NBT 3.2 Fluently add and subtract within 1000 using strategies and algorithms based on place value, properties of operations, and/or the relationship between addition and subtraction.

Materials needed: Worksheet with addition and subtraction problems

Time for lesson: 10-30 minutes

Lesson:

Tell students they are going to practice adding and subtracting, but must also be willing to work as a team.

- Separate students into even teams (or explain someone will go twice).

- Hand out the worksheet face down. Explain to students that though this game is about speed, it is also about finding the correct answer.

- Tell students when you say go that they may turn over the worksheets. Only one person can work on a problem at a time and each person can only do one problem before passing the sheet to the next person.

- Have students arrange themselves in the order they would like to work. Say 'go' and let the students work. Once all problems are finished have that team all stand. Remind the other team(s) to keep working because one incorrect answer will keep the game going.

- The first team to finish all the problems with the correct answers is the winner. (This helps students to learn to slow down and check their work).

- Assessment: Assessment should be based on correct answers

Lesson Two

Title: Online Math Mania

Topic: Adding and subtracting within 1000

Objective of lesson: Students will use an online program to practice addition and subtraction skills.

Common Core State Standard used: NBT 3.2 Fluently add and subtract within 1000 using strategies and algorithms based on place value, properties of operations, and/or the relationship between addition and subtraction.

Materials needed: Computer with internet access

Time for lesson: 30 - 45 minutes

Lesson:

- Have students log onto the site
  http://www.sheppardsoftware.com/math.htm

- Have students click the Fruit Shoot app for addition and subtract. Choose for students or allow them to choose timed or relaxed mode to practice basic math skills.

- Have students record scores over time to assess skill growth.

Assessment: Assessment should be based on increasing scores over time.

Lesson One

Title: Tens Up

Topic: Multiplication by 10

Objective of lesson: Students will practice multiplying by 10

Common Core State Standard used: NBT 3.3 Multiply one-digit whole numbers by multiples of 10 in the range 10–90 (e.g., 9 × 80, 5 × 60) using strategies based on place value and properties of operations.

Materials needed: Room for students to sit with heads down

Time for lesson: 5 - 20 minutes

Lesson:

- With a play on the old game heads-up 7-Up, this game requires students to sit with heads down until the teacher or the person who is 'it' taps them gently.

- Once several children have been tapped they will go to the front of the room and answer one '10' multiplication table. If correct, they can sit choose their replacement (through heads down and tapping), but if incorrect they must stay in place for another round.

- Continue as desired.

Assessment: Assessment should be based on getting correct answers.

Lesson Two

Title: Stick 'Em Up

Topic: Multiplication by 10

Objective of lesson: Students will practice multiplying by 10

Common Core State Standard used: NBT 3.3 Multiply one-digit whole numbers by multiples of 10 in the range 10–90 (e.g., 9 × 80, 5 × 60) using strategies based on place value and properties of operations.

Materials needed: Magnetic numbers (several sets)

Time for lesson: 5 minutes - can be used during center time

Lesson:

- Allow students to practice multiplication with '10' using magnetic numbers.

- Allow one partner to create a problem for another to solve. Each taking a turn as a quick warm-up or practice session.

Assessment: Assessment should be based on getting correct answers and participation.

Lesson One

Title: A Fraction of that Please

Topic: Understanding fractions as part of a whole

Objective of lesson: Students will identify parts of a whole as a fraction.

Common Core State Standard used: NFA 3.1 Understand a fraction 1/*b* as the quantity formed by 1 part when *a* whole is partitioned into *b* equal parts; understand a fraction *a*/*b* as the quantity formed by *a* parts of size 1/*b*.

Materials needed: Equally sectioned shapes (per student)

Time for lesson: 20 - 40 minutes per group

Lesson:

- Explain to students that a part of something, like a shape, is a fraction of it.

- Explain that to get the bottom number (denominator) of a fraction we must count how many total pieces of a shape there are. Then, however many we need is the top number (numerator).

- Share the included example.

- Use sectioned shapes to allow students to practice.

Assessment: Assessment should be based on understanding as well as correctly identifying fractions of a whole.

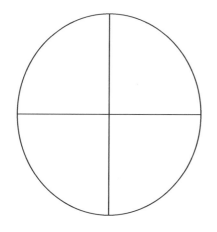

There are four equal sections in this circle so four would be the denominator of the fraction. a/4

Lesson Two

Title: Student Fractions

Topic: Understanding aspects of a fraction

Objective of lesson: Students will use classmates as parts of a fraction, understanding the changes within a fraction.

Common Core State Standard used: NFA 3.1 Understand a fraction $1/b$ as the quantity formed by 1 part when a whole is partitioned into b equal parts; understand a fraction a/b as the quantity formed by a parts of size $1/b$.

Materials needed: Students

Time for lesson: 30 - 45 minutes

Lesson:

- Remind students the parts of a fraction that the denominator represents the total parts of a whole and the numerator is the fraction that is needed or wanted.

- Use all class members as part of the fraction so if 25 students are used it is 25/25 students to represent a whole class.

- Next remove several students and have the class determine what fraction of the students have been removed.

- Try several problems like this and then remove some of the class from the whole and have students change the bottom number of the fraction.

- Try several different arrangements to further understanding. Ex: students wearing different colors, wears glasses, wearing skirts, wearing belts...

Assessment: Assessment should be based on understanding as well as correctly identifying fractions of a whole.

Lesson One

Title: Fractions Rule

Topic: Representing fractions on a number line

Objective of lesson: Students will identify fractions on a ruler or number line.

- Common Core State Standard used: NFA 3.2 Understand a fraction as a number on the number line; represent fractions on a number line diagram.

  - CCSS.Math.Content.3.NF.A.2a Represent a fraction $1/b$ on a number line diagram by defining the interval from 0 to 1 as the whole and partitioning it into b equal parts. Recognize that each part has size $1/b$ and that the endpoint of the part based at 0 locates the number $1/b$ on the number line.

  - CCSS.Math.Content.3.NF.A.2b Represent a fraction a/b on a number line diagram by marking off a lengths $1/b$ from 0. Recognize that the resulting interval has size a/b and that its endpoint locates the number a/b on the number line.

Materials needed: Internet access

Time for lesson: 30 - 45 minutes

Lesson:

- Remind students of the parts of a fraction that the denominator represents the total parts of a whole and the numerator is the fraction that is needed or wanted.

- Explain that almost any item can be split into fraction if desired.

- Help students access http://www.rickyspears.com/rulergame/

- Have students choose timed or untimed and which increment level you desire

Assessment: Assessment should be based on understanding as well as correctly identifying fractions and improvement over time.

Lesson Two

Title: Fractions on a Number Line

Topic: Representing fractions on a number line

Objective of lesson: Students will label fractions on a number line.

Common Core State Standard used: NFA 3.2 Understand a fraction as a number on the number line; represent fractions on a number line diagram.

- CCSS.Math.Content.3.NF.A.2a Represent a fraction $1/b$ on a number line diagram by defining the interval from 0 to 1 as the whole and partitioning it into b equal parts. Recognize that each part has size $1/b$ and that the endpoint of the part based at 0 locates the number $1/b$ on the number line.

- CCSS.Math.Content.3.NF.A.2b Represent a fraction a/b on a number line diagram by marking off a lengths $1/b$ from 0. Recognize that the resulting interval has size a/b and that its endpoint locates the number a/b on the number line.

Materials needed: Overhead or document camera

Marker

Create an unlabeled number line sheet

Time for lesson: 30 - 45 minutes

Lesson:

- Place the number lines on the document camera for the class to see. Explain that each number line is different and asks for a different fraction to be identified.

- Call students one at a time to attempt to place the fraction in the correct place.

Assessment: Assessment should be based on correct placement.

Lesson One

Title: Fraction Fusion

Topic: Understanding fraction equivalents in size

Objective of lesson: Students will practice matching equivalent fractions based on size.

Common Core State Standard used: NFA 3.3 Explain equivalence of fractions in special cases, and compare fractions by reasoning about their size.

- o CCSS.Math.Content.3.NF.A.3a Understand two fractions as equivalent (equal) if they are the same size, or the same point on a number line.

- o CCSS.Math.Content.3.NF.A.3b Recognize and generate simple equivalent fractions, e.g., 1/2 = 2/4, 4/6 = 2/3). Explain why the fractions are equivalent, e.g., by using a visual fraction model.

- o CCSS.Math.Content.3.NF.A.3c Express whole numbers as fractions, and recognize fractions that are equivalent to whole numbers. *Examples: Express 3 in the form 3 = 3/1; recognize that 6/1 = 6; locate 4/4 and 1 at the same point of a number line diagram.*

- o CCSS.Math.Content.3.NF.A.3d Compare two fractions with the same numerator or the same denominator by reasoning about their size. Recognize that comparisons are valid only when the two fractions refer to the same whole. Record the results of comparisons with the symbols >, =, or <, and justify the conclusions, e.g., by using a visual fraction model.

Materials needed: Overhead or document camera

Fractioned shapes (samples included)

Time for lesson: 10-30 minutes

Lesson:

- Place a fractioned shape on the projector and have students identify how many pieces are showing.

- Place the same shape, fractioned differently beside the original shape. Again have students identify how many sections are present.

- Now lay one shape over the other and ask students what the equivalent would be. (Sample below)

- Continue with other shapes and fractional equivalents.

Assessment: Assessment should be based on participation and understanding.

Sample:

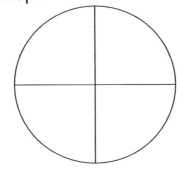   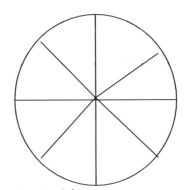

4/4 so one section is 1/4   8/8 so one section is 1/8,

Lesson Two

Title: Fraction Find

Topic: Understanding fraction equivalents in size

Objective of lesson: Students will find equivalents for a given fraction.

Common Core State Standard used: NFA 3.3 Explain equivalence of fractions in special cases, and compare fractions by reasoning about their size.

- o CCSS.Math.Content.3.NF.A.3a Understand two fractions as equivalent (equal) if they are the same size, or the same point on a number line.

- o CCSS.Math.Content.3.NF.A.3b Recognize and generate simple equivalent fractions, e.g., 1/2 = 2/4, 4/6 = 2/3). Explain why the fractions are equivalent, e.g., by using a visual fraction model.

- o CCSS.Math.Content.3.NF.A.3c Express whole numbers as fractions, and recognize fractions that are equivalent to whole numbers. *Examples: Express 3 in the form 3 = 3/1; recognize that 6/1 = 6; locate 4/4 and 1 at the same point of a number line diagram.*

- o CCSS.Math.Content.3.NF.A.3d Compare two fractions with the same numerator or the same denominator by reasoning about their size. Recognize that comparisons are valid only when the two fractions refer to the same whole. Record the results of comparisons with the symbols >, =, or <, and justify the conclusions, e.g., by using a visual fraction model.

Materials needed: Projector hooked to computer

Internet access (per student if not working as a class)

Time for lesson: 15 - 30 minutes

Lesson:

- Share with students that all fractions have an equivalent, something that is equal.

- Help students navigate to http://www.mathsisfun.com/numbers/fraction-number-line.html

- Each time you call out a fraction, have students move the line to that fraction and list or share any equivalents.

- Repeat as desired.

Assessment: Assessment should be based on participation and understanding.

Lesson One

Title: Time We'll Tell

Topic: Telling time on a convention (not digital) clock

Objective of lesson: Students will show and tell time on an analog clock.

Common Core State Standard used: MDA 3.1 Tell and write time to the nearest minute and measure time intervals in minutes. Solve word problems involving addition and subtraction of time intervals in minutes, e.g., by representing the problem on a number line diagram.

Materials needed: Velcro dartboard (directions included)

Moveable analog clock with hands

Area to hang dartboard

Time for lesson: 15 - 25 minutes (per group)

Lesson: (Small groups are best)

- Using a Velcro dartboard, allow students to shoot two darts. The first dart will represent the hour with the second representing the minutes.

- After a child has thrown two darts, then they must represent the time on the clock.

- Have children read the time aloud.

- Allow each child several attempts to practice time.

Assessment: Assessment should be based on participation and understanding.

Dart Board Directions: (Some Velcro dartboards may be available for purchase)

This is not a traditional dartboard as it is just for time telling purposes.

Cover a large square piece of cardboard in felt.

Using a marker or paint, paint the numbers 1-12 on the felt, spaced evenly, and in random order.

Place large Velcro squares under each number (This is what the darts will stick to)

To make darts place small Velcro circles (opposite side of what is on the board) onto flat dart ends which can be purchased at craft stores.

Lesson Two

Title: Time It

Topic: Word problems using time

Objective of lesson: Students will answer questions involving time.

Common Core State Standard used: MDA 3.1 Tell and write time to the nearest minute and measure time intervals in minutes. Solve word problems involving addition and subtraction of time intervals in minutes, e.g., by representing the problem on a number line diagram.

Materials needed: Worksheet (samples included)

Moveable analog clock with hands (per child)

Time for lesson: 20 - 30 minutes

Lesson:

- Place the worksheet on the projector for all to view.

- Have students practice a few times on the clock to make sure students know how to display time appropriately.

- Have the class work through one word problem at a time, displaying the answer on their individual clocks.

Assessment: Assessment should be based on participation and display of correct times.

Sample Problems:

1) Andy is having a party at 2:00PM, but that is not for another 45 minutes. What time is it now?

2) School started three hours and 15 minutes ago. It is now 12:30PM. What time did school start today?

3) The clock shows 1:15. The last time I checked the clock was 47 minutes ago. What time was it when I checked the clock before?

4) Surgery takes a long time. In fact this surgery will take 8 hours and 18 minutes. It is now 6:02 in the morning. What time will this surgery end?

5) I fell asleep after soccer practice. It was 4:19 when I fell asleep and I have been asleep for 2 hours and 16 minutes. What time is it now?

6) The library is opened for 3 hours and 30 minutes before it closes for lunch. If the library opens at 9:00 AM, what time is lunch?

7) Sabrina is taking a timed test that takes 2 hours and 10 minutes. The test started at 8:17. When will it end?

Lesson One

Title: Liquid Estimates

Topic: Estimating liquid volumes

Objective of lesson: Students will estimate liquid volume with a measured comparative.

Common Core State Standard used: MDA 3.2 Measure and estimate liquid volumes and masses of objects using standard units of grams (g), kilograms (kg), and liters (l).[1] Add, subtract, multiply, or divide to solve one-step word problems involving masses or volumes that are given in the same units, e.g., by using drawings (such as a beaker with a measurement scale) to represent the problem.

Materials needed: Marked beakers

Unmarked containers that will hold water

Access to water

Time for lesson: 15 - 20 minutes (per group)

Lesson: (Easiest in small groups)

- Fill several beakers to differing levels and display for students. (Using colored water often helps)

- Have students read the levels of each beaker.

- Next, pour water into several other containers and have students estimate the volume of the water in the new containers.

- After students have recorded estimates, allow them to use an empty beaker to actually measure the volume.

- Compare to estimates, by allowing students to discuss why they estimated what they did.

Assessment: Assessment should be based on participation and appropriate estimates with improvement over time.

Lesson Two

Title: Weigh Your Options

Topic: Estimating small weights

Objective of lesson: Students will estimate weights

Common Core State Standard used: MDA 3.2 Measure and estimate liquid volumes and masses of objects using standard units of grams (g), kilograms (kg), and liters (l).[1] Add, subtract, multiply, or divide to solve one-step word problems involving masses or volumes that are given in the same units, e.g., by using drawings (such as a beaker with a measurement scale) to represent the problem.

Materials needed: Small weight set with balance or scale

Access to numerous small objects

Time for lesson: 15 - 20 minutes (per group)

Lesson: (Easiest in small groups)

- Allow students to explore weights by picking them up and feeling the weight, placing them on the balance or scale and comparing weights.

- Next tell students that they are going to estimate the weights of several small objects.

- Show students the first object. If they wish allow them to pick it up and compare it to the weights in their hand.

- Have students record an estimated weight.

- Allow one person in the group to actually measure the small object.

- Review estimates for accuracy.

- Repeat with several objects.

Assessment: Assessment should be based on participation and appropriate estimates with improvement over time.

Lesson One

Title: Scale That Building

Topic: Drawing objects to scale

Objective of lesson: Students will draw various objects to scale.

Common Core State Standard used: MDA 3.3 Draw a scaled picture graph and a scaled bar graph to represent a data set with several categories. Solve one- and two-step "how many more" and "how many less" problems using information presented in scaled bar graphs. *For example, draw a bar graph in which each square in the bar graph might represent 5 pets.*

Materials needed: Graph paper

Colored pencils

List of objects to draw to scale

Time for lesson: 30 - 45 minutes

Lesson:

- Give each student a sheet of large graph paper.

- Demonstrate that if each square represents one foot then a building that was 20 feet tall and ten feet wide would go up 20 squares and across ten squares.

- Demonstrate again with an object that is only 6 inches tall such as an apple beside the building.

- Explain that these objects are drawn to scale.

- Offer students a list of objects with the height and width of each object.

- Allow students to draw, label, and color each scale item.

Assessment: Assessment should be based on drawing items to scale appropriately.

Lesson Two

Title: Raise The Bar

Topic: Creating bar graphs

Objective of lesson: Students will create bar graphs with given information.

Common Core State Standard used: MDA 3.3 Draw a scaled picture graph and a scaled bar graph to represent a data set with several categories. Solve one- and two-step "how many more" and "how many less" problems using information presented in scaled bar graphs. *For example, draw a bar graph in which each square in the bar graph might represent 5 pets.*

Materials needed: Graph paper

Colored pencils

Time for lesson: 40 - 50 minutes

Lesson:

- Show students how to properly label and number a graph that goes up to the number 25 on the x axis.

- Have students label the y axis with the different types (not numbers) of pets that students in the class have.

- Now allow students to interview every classmate to learn how many of each pet type they have. For each of the pet type that a student has, one square should be colored in on the graph.

- Remind students to put their own data on the chart and use different colors for each pet type.

- Have students complete the rest of the graph. Labels, names, intervals …

Assessment: Assessment should be based on creating an accurate bar graph and answering questions correctly.

Lesson One

Title: Do You Measure Up

Topic: Measuring to parts of an inch

Objective of lesson: Students will measure specified objects to fractions of an inch.

Common Core State Standard used: MDA 3.4 Generate measurement data by measuring lengths using rulers marked with halves and fourths of an inch. Show the data by making a line plot, where the horizontal scale is marked off in appropriate units— whole numbers, halves, or quarters.

Materials needed: Rulers

Paper

Pencil

List of classroom objects to measure

Time for lesson: 30 - 45 minutes

Lesson:

- Remind students of how to read a ruler using $\frac{1}{4}$ inch demarcations.

- Explain that they are going to measure certain objects in the room and then rank them according to length.

- Offer students a list of objects around the room or write the list on the board.

- Allow students to measure and record lengths of the given objects.

- After all lengths have been recorded have students rank the objects from shortest to longest.

- Have students work with partners and check answers. If they have different answers they need to go back to the object and remeasure the object.

Assessment: Assessment should be based on accurately measuring and recording lengths to the closest $\frac{1}{4}$ inch.

Lesson Two

Title: Looking For Length

Topic: Measuring to parts of an inch

Objective of lesson: Students will measure objects to fractions of an inch.

Common Core State Standard used: MDA 3.4 Generate measurement data by measuring lengths using rulers marked with halves and fourths of an inch. Show the data by making a line plot, where the horizontal scale is marked off in appropriate units— whole numbers, halves, or quarters.

Materials needed: Rulers

Paper

Pencil

Time for lesson: 30-60 minutes

Lesson:

- Remind students of how to read a ruler using $\frac{1}{4}$ inch demarcations.

- Explain to students that they are going to go on a length treasure hunt.

- Give students 5 to 10 lengths that they need to find in the designated area. (This is fun outdoors).

- Remind students that the length has to be measured to the $\frac{1}{4}$ and has to be as close as possible, but not exact.

- Allow students to look around and measure random objects and as a particular length is found, have students write the length and object found to match the length the closest.

Assessment: Assessment should be based on finding objects to match the given lengths.

Lesson One

Title: Inching Along

Topic: Measuring using a pre-designated unit of measure

Objective of lesson: Students will use a unit measure to assess surface area.

Common Core State Standard used: MDA 3.5 Recognize area as an attribute of plane figures and understand concepts of area measurement.

- CCSS.Math.Content.3.MD.C.5a A square with side length 1 unit, called "a unit square," is said to have "one square unit" of area, and can be used to measure area.

- CCSS.Math.Content.3.MD.C.5b A plane figure which can be covered without gaps or overlaps by n unit squares is said to have an area of n square units.

Materials needed: 1 inch square 'units' (blocks)

Larger, perfectly square blocks (often contained in math sets)

Time for lesson: 30 - 45 minutes

Lesson:

- Hold up the 1 inch square for students and explain that it is 1 square inch and it is the 'unit' by which they will measure today.

- Have students place the unit on the other sized squares to determine how many units make up a whole.

- Repeat for each larger square.

- Students can work in small groups and challenge each other with other size squares.

Assessment: Assessment should be based on using units to measure as well as participation.

Lesson Two

Title: Carpeting Creation

Topic: Measuring area

Objective of lesson: Students will measure and calculate area

Common Core State Standard used: MDA 3.5 Recognize area as an attribute of plane figures and understand concepts of area measurement.

- CCSS.Math.Content.3.MD.C.5a A square with side length 1 unit, called "a unit square," is said to have "one square unit" of area, and can be used to measure area.

- CCSS.Math.Content.3.MD.C.5b A plane figure which can be covered without gaps or overlaps by n unit squares is said to have an area of n square units.

Materials needed: Tape measure

Rooms to measure

Drawing paper – optional

Time for lesson: 30 - 40 minutes

Lesson:

- Explain to students that measuring area is something that will be used often as they grow older. Share times when measuring area is needed, carpeting, tiling, rearranging a room.

- Tell students that they are going to pretend to be builders and will work in pairs to calculate the area of the classroom for new tiles.

- Allow students to work together to measure the area.

- Now explain that each tile is one foot square and they come in boxes of 10 tiles. Ask how many tiles and how many boxes will be needed.

- Help students think though the process of how to figure the number of needed boxes of tile.

- Students may draw a picture if this helps them visualize the problem.

- After the first problem, have students create their own with a partner. Then they can pair share with another group.

Assessment: Assessment should be based on correct measuring and assessment of how much tile would be needed.

Lesson One

Title: Use What is Available

Topic: Using improvised measuring units to determine area

Objective of lesson: Students will improvise units to measure a given surface.

Common Core State Standard used: MDA 3.6 Measure areas by counting unit squares (square cm, square m, square in, square ft, and improvised units).

Materials needed: Assortment of objects such as blocks, shoes, pencils, etc.

Rulers

Time for lesson: 30 - 40 minutes

Lesson:

- Explain to students that measuring area is something that will be used often as they grow older. Share times when measuring area is needed, carpeting, tiling, rearranging a room.

- Tell students that they are going to pretend to be builders and will work in pairs to calculate the area of the classroom for new tiles. Unfortunately, these builders forgot their tape measures.

- Show students the available tools on display and explain that in a pinch you can use anything to measure and then take that object with you to measure, and then figure out a normal unit.

- Have students work together to use the new 'units' to measure a given area.

- After the number of unique 'units' have been calculated have students measure the unit with a ruler.

- After an actual measurement in inches has been found have students figure out the actual length or the area measured in inches or feet.

- Continue with new problems.

Assessment: Assessment should be based on correct measuring and correct conversion of special units to recognized units.

Lesson Two

Title: Online Area Madness

Topic: Using online tools to determine area

Objective of lesson: Students will find the area of specified online drawings

Common Core State Standard used: MDA 3.6 Measure areas by counting unit squares (square cm, square m, square in, square ft, and improvised units).

Materials needed: Computers with Internet access

Paper

Pencil

Time for lesson: 15 - 30 minutes

Lesson: *This can be completed as a class on the white board

- Remind students how to determine area and perimeter.

- Have students log onto
  http://www.mathplayground.com/area_perimeter.html

- First have students read everything in the introduction to understand what is expected. Answer any questions students may have.

- Allow students to attempt several rounds of the provided game to increase measuring and calculating abilities.

Assessment: Assessment should be based on correct answers.

Lesson One

Title: Area Found

Topic: Determining area through addition and multiplication

Objective of lesson: Students will use math blocks to determine area.

Common Core State Standard used: MDA 3.7 Relate area to the operations of multiplication and addition.

- CCSS.Math.Content.3.MD.C.7a Find the area of a rectangle with whole-number side lengths by tiling it, and show that the area is the same as would be found by multiplying the side lengths.

- CCSS.Math.Content.3.MD.C.7b Multiply side lengths to find areas of rectangles with whole-number side lengths in the context of solving real world and mathematical problems, and represent whole-number products as rectangular areas in mathematical reasoning.

- CCSS.Math.Content.3.MD.C.7c Use tiling to show in a concrete case that the area of a rectangle with whole-number side lengths a and $b + c$ is the sum of $a \times b$ and $a \times c$. Use area models to represent the distributive property in mathematical reasoning.

- CCSS.Math.Content.3.MD.C.7d Recognize area as additive. Find areas of rectilinear figures by decomposing them into non-overlapping rectangles and adding the areas of the non-overlapping parts, applying this technique to solve real world problems.

Materials needed: Math blocks of different sizes

Time for lesson: 20 - 30 minutes

Lesson:

- Remind students of the relationship between addition and multiplication. Ex: 3x 3 is the same as 3 + 3 + 3. Explain that this is also true of area.

- Have students use math blocks to count the number of smaller blocks that will fit on the large square. Ask students how they could have figured out the same number without adding. (Multiply)

- Ask what the multiplication problem would be and the answer.

- Repeat with several different sized grid blocks.

Assessment: Assessment should be based on understanding.

Lesson Two

Title: Fencing In Fido

Topic: Determining area through multiplication in real life examples

Objective of lesson: Students will use written descriptions to determine area.

Common Core State Standard used: MDA 3.7 Relate area to the operations of multiplication and addition.

- o CCSS.Math.Content.3.MD.C.7a Find the area of a rectangle with whole-number side lengths by tiling it, and show that the area is the same as would be found by multiplying the side lengths.

- o CCSS.Math.Content.3.MD.C.7b Multiply side lengths to find areas of rectangles with whole-number side lengths in the context of solving real world and mathematical problems, and represent whole-number products as rectangular areas in mathematical reasoning.

- o CCSS.Math.Content.3.MD.C.7c Use tiling to show in a concrete case that the area of a rectangle with whole-number side lengths a and $b + c$ is the sum of $a \times b$ and $a \times c$. Use area models to represent the distributive property in mathematical reasoning.

- o CCSS.Math.Content.3.MD.C.7d Recognize area as additive. Find areas of rectilinear figures by decomposing them into non-overlapping rectangles and adding the areas of the non-overlapping parts, applying this technique to solve real world problems.

Materials needed: Written problems (samples included)

Time for lesson: 20 - 30 minutes

Lesson:

- Remind students of how to find area when the length and width are known for an object.

- Share the included story with students about fencing in a yard for a new puppy.

- Have students solve for area each time it is questioned in the short story.

Assessment: Assessment should be based on correct calculations.

Sam and Abby had finally talked their parents into a new puppy. They had visited the shelter many times and knew exactly which puppy they wanted to adopt. Sam and Abby's dad reminded them that the puppy would need a safe place to play outdoors so a fence was needed. They would need to figure out how much fence needed to be purchased. Sam and Abby worked together to measure the yard and found that it was 12 feet long and 8 feet wide. What was the area? After thinking about it, Sam and Abby's mom did not want the new puppy to destroy her flowers that were on half the lawn, so she asked them to measure again and exclude the part of the yard with her flowers. The new measurements were 7 feet long and 5 feet wide. What was the area? Right before going to the store to buy fencing, Abby and Sam's dad found out a large dog park was available right around the corner. He made Abby and Sam agree to take the puppy at least once a day to play. This meant the puppy only needed a pen in the back yard to go out and enjoy the weather when no one was home. So Sam and Abby had to measure once again for a pen to be build. This time the measurements were 6 feet long and 3 feet wide. What was the area? Shortly after the pen was built a new puppy came to live with Sam and Abby. They named him Sparky.

Lesson One

Title: Venture into the Unknown

Topic: Finding area with an unknown side

Objective of lesson: Students will find unknown side lengths

Common Core State Standard used: MDA 3.8 Solve real world and mathematical problems involving perimeters of polygons, including finding the perimeter given the side lengths, finding an unknown side length, and exhibiting rectangles with the same perimeter and different areas or with the same area and different perimeters.

Materials needed: Sample area problems

Time for lesson: 30 - 40 minutes

Lesson:

- Remind students of how to find area of a rectangle. Ask students what could be done if one of the numbers was missing but you had the total area?

- Offer the following example. A yard was fenced in to prepare for a new pet. The total area was 40 square feet. The length of the yard was 8 feet. What was the width?

- Explain that since we know the total a problem can be written as such 8 x ____ = 40.

- Allow students to try several problems on their own.

Assessment: Assessment should be based on correct answers.

Sample Problems:

8 feet

Total 48 sq ft

3 feet

Total 21 sq ft

10 feet

Total 50 sq ft

2 feet

Total 6 sq ft

4 feet

Total 28 sq ft

9 feet

Total 54 sq ft

Lesson Two

Title: Propensity for Perimeters

Topic: Finding perimeter

Objective of lesson: Students will find perimeters of shapes.

Common Core State Standard used: MDA 3.8 Solve real world and mathematical problems involving perimeters of polygons, including finding the perimeter given the side lengths, finding an unknown side length, and exhibiting rectangles with the same perimeter and different areas or with the same area and different perimeters.

Materials needed: Variety of recognizable shapes

Paper

Pencil

Rulers

Time for lesson: 30 - 45 minutes

Lesson:

- Remind students that adding the length of all sides of an object will add up to the perimeter of that object.

- Offer students several flat shapes to measure all sides. Make sure students record the length of each side as it is measured.

- Have students calculate the perimeter of each provided shape.

- Students can draw shapes in their math journal and share with a partner or small group for practice.

Assessment: Assessment should be based correct measuring and calculating.

Lesson One

Title: Shape Sort

Topic: Categorizing shapes

Objective of lesson: Students will group shapes according to traits.

Common Core State Standard used: GA 3.1 Understand that shapes in different categories (e.g., rhombuses, rectangles, and others) may share attributes (e.g., having four sides), and that the shared attributes can define a larger category (e.g., quadrilaterals). Recognize rhombuses, rectangles, and squares as examples of quadrilaterals, and draw examples of quadrilaterals that do not belong to any of these subcategories.

Materials needed: Variety of recognizable shapes

Paper

Pencil

Time for lesson: 5 minutes (per group) 15 minutes – whole group

Lesson: (Small groups)

- Explain to students that sometimes shapes fit into many different categories. Shapes could be sorted by size, number of sides, dimensions, even color.

- Tell students that when you start the timer they will have 5 minutes to sort their shapes into as many categories as they can think of. Once each category is approved they can write it and try to find another one. Each category must contain at least two of the shared shapes.

- Repeat with each group. Share all categories on the board and ask students to try to sort shapes into the categories.

Assessment: Assessment should be based finding at least three separate categories.

Lesson Two

Title: Quadrilateral Quandary

Topic: Identifying quadrilaterals

Objective of lesson: Students will identify quadrilaterals with accuracy.

Common Core State Standard used: GA 3.1 Understand that shapes in different categories (e.g., rhombuses, rectangles, and others) may share attributes (e.g., having four sides), and that the shared attributes can define a larger category (e.g., quadrilaterals). Recognize rhombuses, rectangles, and squares as examples of quadrilaterals, and draw examples of quadrilaterals that do not belong to any of these subcategories.

Materials needed: Computer with Internet access

Time for lesson: 10-20 minutes

Lesson:

- Remind students of the definition of a quadrilateral. Explain that they are going to play a game in which they must identify particular quadrilaterals within a game. Each type will be described before it must be identified.

- Allow students to log onto http://cemc2.math.uwaterloo.ca/mathfrog/english/kidz/Games4.shtml

- Have students click on Call of Geometry: Quadrilateral Warfare to play the game of identifying quadrilaterals.

- Great to use as center time once they have been introduced to the program.

Assessment: Assessment should be based on score of accuracy.

Lesson One

Title: Partitioned Parts

Topic: Partitioning areas into equal parts

Objective of lesson: Students will partition parts in equal sections.

Common Core State Standard used: GA 3.2 Partition shapes into parts with equal areas. Express the area of each part as a unit fraction of the whole. *For example, partition a shape into 4 parts with equal area, and describe the area of each part as 1/4 of the area of the shape.*

Materials needed: Paper shapes

Scissors

Ruler

Pencil

Time for lesson: 30 - 45 minutes

Lesson:

- Have students first measure the area of a given shape and write the total in the center of that shape.

- Next tell students how many parts you wish to have the shape divided into (make sure the total is equally divisible by that number).

- Have students measure and cut the shape into the equal number of pieces requested.

- Have students measure the new area for the pieces. Each piece should be identical and if added the areas should equal the original total.

- Continue with more shapes.

- Students can draw more shapes in their journals and measure and place the area in the middle of the shape.

Assessment: Assessment should be based on correctly calculating area and cutting shapes.

Lesson Two

Title: Parts Art

Topic: Recognizing equal parts of a given shape

Objective of lesson: Students will create art with pieces of a given shape.

Common Core State Standard used: GA 3.2 Partition shapes into parts with equal areas. Express the area of each part as a unit fraction of the whole. *For example, partition a shape into 4 parts with equal area, and describe the area of each part as 1/4 of the area of the shape.*

Materials needed: Math pattern blocks

Time for lesson: 5-10 minutes

Lesson:

- Offer children an assortment of pattern blocks. Explain that each of these blocks can be partitioned into equal sections.

- Have students lay a large yellow octagon on their desk and see what other shapes fit equally into the larger one.

- Have students find at least two to three options for the larger shapes.

- Explain that if two blue shapes make up on yellow shape they are each $\frac{1}{2}$ the size. If 4 shapes equally fill the yellow shape then they are $\frac{1}{4}$ the size, etc.

Assessment: Assessment should be based on understanding and correct partitioning.

Rubrics: These rubrics are generic and can be altered to fit any assignment that is needed, as desired.

4 – Exceeds Standard   3 – Meets Standard   2 – Approaching Standard

1 – Below Standard

Writing

CATEGORY	4	3	2	1
Focus on Topic (Content)	There is one clear, well-focused topic. Main idea stands out and is supported by interesting details.	Main idea is clear but the supporting details are general.	Main idea is somewhat clear but there is a need for more supporting details.	The main idea is not clear. There is a seemingly random collection of details.
Sentence Fluency	All sentences are well-constructed with varied structure.	Most sentences are well-constructed with varied structure.	Some sentences are not well-constructed and may be similar in structure.	Sentences lack structure or appear incomplete or rambling.
Capitalization & Punctuation (Conventions)	Writer makes no errors in capitalization, or punctuation, so the paper is exceptionally easy to read.	Writer makes 1 or 2 errors in capitalization or punctuation, but the paper is still easy to read.	Writer makes a few errors in capitalization and/or punctuation that catch the reader's attention and interrupt the flow.	Writer makes several errors in capitalization and/or punctuation that catch the reader's attention and greatly interrupt the flow.
Spelling	Writer makes no errors spelling that distract the reader from the content.	Writer makes 1-2 errors in spelling that distract the reader from the content.	Writer makes 3-4 errors in spelling that distract the reader from the content.	Writer makes more than 4 errors in spelling that distract the reader from the content.
Writes legibly	Paper is very neatly written with no distracting corrections.	Paper is mostly neatly written with 1 or 2 distracting corrections (e.g., dark cross-outs; bumpy white-out, words written over).	The writing is somewhat messy and the reader has to work hard to read the paper.	The writing is mostly unreadable and the reader has to work hard to read the paper.

4 – Exceeds Standard   3 – Meets Standard   2 – Approaching Standard

1 – Below Standard

Speaking

CATEGORY	4	3	2	1
Quality of Work	Provided work of the highest quality.	Provided high quality work.	Provided work that occasionally needs to be checked/redone by other group members to ensure quality.	Provided work that usually needs to be checked/redone by others to ensure quality.
Focus on the task	Stayed focused on the task and what needed to be done. Very self-directed.	Focused on the task and what needed to be done most of the time.	Focused on the task and what needed to be done some of the time.	Rarely focused on the task and what needed to be done. Lets others do the work.
Content	Work included all that was required to be complete	Work included most of the information needed to be complete.	Work included some of the work that needed to be included.	Work included a little of the information that was required to be a complete assignment.
Speech	Student maintained a level of speech that was proper for the audience (proper speech and vocabulary).	Student often maintained a level of speech that was necessary for the audience (very little slang).	Student sometimes used slang words & sometimes used proper vocabulary.	Student used mostly slang and very little proper speech.
Posture	Students maintained a proper posture the whole time (didn't slouch of lean against a wall/chair.)	Students maintained a proper posture most of the time (didn't slouch of lean against a wall/chair.)	Students maintained a proper posture some of the time while slouching or leaning against a wall/chair.	Students rarely maintained a good posture (slouching or leaning).

5 – Exceeds Standards 4 – Above Standard   3 – Meets Standard

2 – Approaching Standard   1 – Below Standard

Group Work

CATEGORY	5	4	3	2	1
Cooperation with others	Works well with others and even encourages other group members.	Works well with others.	Did what they were supposed to do, but nothing more.	Works in group, but is often reluctant when asked to do something.	Argues and prevents progress completely.
Voluntary Participation	Willing to be a part of group and initiates activity.	Participates willingly and follows directions.	Participates minimally.	Doesn't participate voluntarily, but does participate when addressed.	Does not participate at all, even when addressed.
Overall Work Quality	Performs work at an exceptional quality. Student also turns work in on time and doesn't fall behind. Final product exceeded expectations.	Performs quality work. Student also turns work in on time and doesn't fall behind. Final work met expectations.	Fell a little behind, but did eventually turn work in. Final work met expectations.	Work completed was at a minimal level of expectation.	Student failed to complete assignments and final product failed to meet expectations.
Conflict Resolution	Never involved in significant debate or conflict.	Involved in minor group dispute, but resolved it quickly and reasonably. Dispute did not affect attitude of group or quality of work.	Involved in group dispute but it was resolved without teacher.	Involved in group dispute that had to be resolved by teacher intervention.	Student had to be referred to dean or removed from group due to a conflict during collaborative activity.
Overall Attitude	Positive asset to group, uplifting attitude and easy to collaborate with.	Quiet hard worker who is easy to work with.	Quiet individual. Shyness made it difficult to complete the tasks.	Difficult Student to work with, but did get his or her work complete.	Difficult student in group. Would not be willing to work with this individual in the future.

Editing

CATEGORY				
Focus on Topic (Content)	There is one clear, well-focused topic. Main idea stands out and is supported by detailed information. - MEANINGFUL TITLE	The topic appropriate for the length of the paper- there is enough information to fulfill the assignment	Topic sentences are clear - you know what the paragraph will be about	The topic is developed enough to keep the reader's attention and appropriate for the audience
Opening paragraph	Strong beginning sentence	Facts included about the main topic	Beginning paragraph pulls the reader in and wants them to read on	Ending sentences that leads into the rest of the paper- possibly your opinion when appropriate
Sentences	No run-on sentences	The sentences make sense and are related to the main topic- effective word choice	Sentences contain important details- no "fluff"	Smooth transitions from one sentence to another
Paragraphs	Paragraphs have a beginning and concluding sentence	Paragraphs are organized and flow- I read the paper out loud	Appropriate language being used for the paper	Paragraphs support the central idea
Grammar	All words are capitalized properly	Use quotations properly	Spelling errors or usage errors	Punctuation is used correctly- not overused or not used enough
Conclusion paragraph	Strong conclusion	Wrap up the paper and pull the paragraphs together	Make sure to really get your point across at this time	Conclusion pulls together the meaning of the paper and purpose
Final editing	Strong and meaningful title which tells the reader what the paper is about	PROPER CITATIONS of all material researched from other sources- no plagiarizing	Name, date, teachers name on the paper	read the paper out loud again to check for mistakes possibly missed before

4 – Exceeds Standard   3 – Meets Standard   2 – Approaching Standard

1 – Below Standard

Artwork (landscape)

CATEGORY	4	3	2	1
Drawing	Drawing is expressive and detailed. Shapes, patterns, shading and/or texture are used to add interest to the painting. Student has great control and is able to experiment a little.	Drawing is expressive and somewhat detailed. Little use has been made of pattern, shading, or texture. Student has basics, but had not "branched" out.	Drawing has few details. It is primarily representational with very little use of pattern, shading or texture. Student needs to improve control.	The drawing lacks almost all detail or it is unclear what the drawing is intended to be. Student needs to work on control.
Color Choices	Choice and application of color shows an advanced knowledge of color relationships. Color choice enhances the idea being expressed.	Choice and application of color shows knowledge of color relationships. Colors are appropriate for the idea being expressed.	Choice and application of color shows knowledge of color relationships. Colors are, however, NOT appropriate for the idea being expressed.	Student needs to work on learning color relationships and using that knowledge in his/her work.
Use of materials	Student typically keeps painting materials and area clean and protected without reminders. The student shows great respect for the materials and his fellow students.	Student typically adequately cleans materials and work area at the end of the session without reminder, but the area may be messy during the work session. Student shows respect for materials and fellow students.	Student adequately cleans and takes care of materials if reminded. Occasional spills and messy work area may be seen. Shows some respect for materials and fellow students.	Student deliberately misuses materials and/or does not adequately clean materials or area when reminded. Shows little respect for materials or fellow students.
Time/Effort	Class time was used wisely. Much time and effort went into the planning and design of the mask. It is clear the student worked at home as well as at school.	Class time was used wisely. Student could have put in more time and effort at home.	Class time was not always used wisely, but student did do some additional work at home.	Class time was not used wisely and the student put in no additional effort.

4 – Exceeds Standard   3 – Meets Standard   2 – Approaching Standard

1 – Below Standard

Interviewing

CATEGORY	4	3	2	1
Organization	The student was clear in the introduction, used the appropriate questions to illicit the most information.	The student was able to gain some knowledge of the problem.	Interview had some focus but was unable to establish the scope of the problem. Questions were not organized.	No apparent organization. Failed to identify the problem in any legal context.
Knowledge Gained	Student can accurately answer several questions about the person who was interviewed and can tell how this interview relates to the material being studied in class.	Student can accurately answer a few questions about the person who was interviewed and can tell how this interview relates to the material being studied in class.	Student can accurately answer a few questions about the person who was interviewed.	Student cannot accurately answer questions about the person who was interviewed.
Follow-up Questions	The student listened carefully to the person being interviewed and asked several relevant follow-up questions based on what the person said and engaged in "active listening."	The student listened carefully to the person being interviewed and asked a couple of relevant follow-up questions based on what the person said and was somewhat engaged in listening.	The student asked a couple of follow-up questions based on what the student thought the person said and often repeated questions that were previously asked.	The student did not ask any follow-up questions based on what the person said but proceeded to ask a series of leading questions which produced limited results.
Open-Ended Questions	The student asked open-ended questions in an attempt to gain the most information.	Student asked a couple of open ended questions but proceeded to ask more leading questions before asking follow-up questions.	The student asked one opening questions and failed to ask any additional opening questions when different subjects were discussed.	Asked exclusively open-ended questions without an identifiable sequence.
Note taking	The interviewer took occasional notes during the interview, but usually maintained focus on the person rather than the notes. Notes were added to immediately after the interview so facts were not lost.	The interviewer took occasional notes during the interview, but usually maintained focus on the person rather than the notes. No additional notes were taken.	The interviewer took notes during the interview, but did so in a way that interrupted the "flow" of the interview. Additional notes may, or may not, have been taken.	The interviewer took no notes during or after the interview.

4 – Exceeds Standard   3 – Meets Standard   2 – Approaching Standard

1 – Below Standard

Brochure Making

CATEGORY	4	3	2	1
Writing - Organization	Each section in the brochure has a clear beginning, middle, and end.	Almost all sections of the brochure have a clear beginning, middle and end.	Half of the sections of the brochure have a clear beginning, middle and end.	Less than half of the sections of the brochure have a clear beginning, middle and end.
Writing - Grammar	There are no grammatical mistakes in the brochure.	There are no grammatical mistakes in the brochure after feedback from an adult.	There are 1-2 grammatical mistakes in the brochure even after feedback from an adult.	There are several grammatical mistakes in the brochure even after feedback from an adult.
Spelling & Proofreading	No spelling errors remain after one person other than the typist reads and corrects the brochure.	No more than 2 spelling error remains after one person other than the typist reads and corrects the brochure.	No more than 3 spelling errors remain after one person other than the typist reads and corrects the brochure.	Several spelling errors in the brochure.
Writing - Vocabulary	The author correctly uses several new words and defines words unfamiliar to the reader.	The author correctly uses a few new words and defines words unfamiliar to the reader.	The author tries to use some new vocabulary, but may use 1-2 words incorrectly.	The authors do not incorporate new vocabulary.
Writing - Mechanics	Capitalization and punctuation are correct throughout the brochure.	Most capitalization and punctuation are correct throughout the brochure.	There are 3 – 4 capitalization and/or punctuation errors in the brochure.	There are several capitalization or punctuation errors in the brochure.
Content - Accuracy	All facts in the brochure are accurate.	99-90% of the facts in the brochure are accurate.	89-80% of the facts in the brochure are accurate.	Fewer than 80% of the facts in the brochure are accurate.
Attractiveness & Organization	The brochure has exceptionally attractive formatting and well-organized information.	The brochure has attractive formatting and well-organized information.	The brochure has well-organized information.	The brochure's formatting and organization of material are confusing to the reader.
Graphics/Pictures	Graphics go well with the content and there is a good mix of text and graphics.	Graphics go well with the content, but there are so many pictures that they distract from the text.	Graphics go well with the content, but there are too few and the brochure is mostly writing.	Graphics do not go with the information.

CCSS Lesson Plan Books – K – Fifth grade

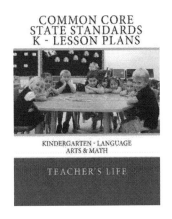

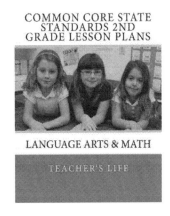

These lesson plan books and other products also sold at

www.myteacherslife.com

24426871R00119